Godmanchester:

A Celebration of 800 Years

To Pat
best wishes from
Pam & Ken Sneath.

Godmanchester:

A Celebration of 800 Years

Pam and Ken Sneath

With a Foreword by
the Mayor of Godmanchester

EAH Press — Cambridge

EAH Press
7 Thornton Court
Thornton Road
Girton
Cambridge CB3 ONS

First published in Great Britain in 2011

Cover design by
Blue Ocean Publishing, Cambridge

Printed in Great Britain by
MPG Biddles Limited, Kings Lynn

ISBN 978-0-9560384-4-9

This book is dedicated to the people of Godmanchester who warmly welcomed us when we arrived thirty years ago and among whom we have made so many good friends.

TABLE OF CONTENTS

ACKNOWLEDGEMENTS

We are indebted to the work of Chris Stringer, the Ancient Human Occupation of Britain Project (AHOB), Michael Green, Tim Malim and the former Archaeological Field Unit of Cambridgeshire County Council for much of the material for chapters two and three. Many people have lent us documents and aided our research, including Vera Arnold, Alan and Lesley Akeroyd, Roger Brudenell, Bob Burn-Murdoch, Quinton Carroll, Mary Carter, Beth Davis, Michael Green, Alan Hooker, Marion Hyde, John Leach, Madelaine Liddiard, Gary Oddie, Nick and Neil Pedlar, Gerald Reeve, David Stokes and Christopher Vane Percy. A number of residents have invited us into their homes and kindly granted permission to take photographs of their houses and gardens. We are grateful to those who have commented on the draft text, in particular Evelyn Lord, Jo Sear and Tim Sneath and also to Graham Campbell for drawing the map. They bear no responsibility for any remaining errors.

Most of the photographs included in the book were taken by the authors. We are grateful to those who have granted permission for their copyright photographs and illustrations to be used including Huntingdonshire Archives and Local Studies, Norris Museum, Porch Museum, Cambridgeshire County Council, Gospel Standard Library, Michael Green, Alan Hooker, Gary Oddie, Gerald Reeve, Graham Reynolds and Christopher Vane Percy.

Godmanchester, April 2011

FOREWORD

The year 2012 is an important milestone in the history of Godmanchester for it celebrates the 800th anniversary of our town. In 1212 King John granted Godmanchester its first Charter and a measure of self-government. It is from such beginnings that our present Town Council has evolved. It is fitting that we celebrate this important anniversary and so together with the Community Association, the Town Council will be organising a series of events for the whole community.

I particularly welcome this publication which will help to inform our celebrations. Our town has a long and fascinating history and its story deserves a wide audience. Pam and Ken Sneath have spent a number of years researching Godmanchester's history from a wide range of primary sources. They have been assisted by many of our residents and the result of this collaborative venture will become an important record of the community for many years to come.

Alan Welton
Mayor of Godmanchester

April 2011

PREFACE

This book is written to celebrate the 800th anniversary of Godmanchester's charter granted by King John in 1212. It seeks to cover an ambitious time frame and we are inevitably reliant on the expertise of others as well as our own. This requires no apology, for recovering the past is a collaborative effort. Ken's specialism is social and economic history and in particular the history of the seventeenth and eighteenth centuries. Pam has studied archaeology. Historians and archaeologists do not always co-operate but when they do each can benefit from the other. The written records beloved by historians are often illuminated by the artefacts uncovered by archaeologists. And those artefacts are set in context by the records. Furthermore we would know very little about the earliest period of our town's history without the contribution of archaeology.

The Causeway, Godmanchester

Many readers of this book will have walked past this sign in Godmanchester and perhaps not noticed it. It is placed on a building in The Causeway. In a simple and humorous way it captures one of the dilemmas of history. Something happens every day but is it significant or important? The historian makes that judgement and in so doing creates history. Whether or not you agree with our interpretations of what is significant in the history of our town, we hope that you will enjoy this account of its story.

1

INTRODUCTION

If you stand on the Chinese Bridge in the centre of Godmanchester you are perfectly placed to take in the town's history. Behind you flows the River Great Ouse and along this river valley the first people came to this region. They were hunters and gatherers and the river provided a rich source of food and a relatively easy means to travel.

Look ahead and you can see the junction of Cambridge Street and The Causeway. These roads roughly follow what were once the Roman walls. The site of the North Gate of the Roman town can just be seen on the right hand side of the road as it heads off towards the A14. The name Godmanchester is an immediate reminder that this was once a Roman town. It had an inn and baths where travellers could be refreshed and horses stabled. In the centre of the town stood a Roman fort built very soon after the Roman conquest.

Turn to your right and you will see the Mill Lade. This was the work of the Danes who occupied the town in the ninth century. But in the first part of the next century they were driven northwards and it was the Anglo-Saxon King, Edward the Elder who was responsible for changing the road system which survives to the present day. After Edward, no longer did the main road pass through the centre of the town but now followed broadly where the walls had stood.

The Iron Age peoples once worshipped the river god Abandinus here. Look a little further to your right along the Causeway and you can see the children's nursery before the corner of Pinfold Lane. Just behind the nursery under Granary Close lies a Roman Temple which may have become the sanctuary for the town's river god. When the Roman Emperor Constantine converted to Christianity in the fourth century he made it the state religion. It was not long before Abandinus and the Roman gods Venus and Mercury were replaced by the Christian God. Towering above Post Street the spire of the church witnesses to that change as it soars upwards from the highest point of the town. Although the present tower only dates from the seventeenth century, a church has stood on this spot for much more than a millennium.

Look to your left and you see the Queen Elizabeth School which dates from the sixteenth century. Here the town's most famous son Stephen Marshall went to school. He was an important figure in the momentous events of the Civil War which convulsed the nation. In the school the Porch Museum has many artefacts which survive to illustrate the history of the town. At the time of writing, a copy of the town's charter of 1212 hangs proudly on one of the walls in the school. It is this charter which this book celebrates. But to properly understand the history of our town we must now travel almost a million years backwards in time to when the first hominids appeared in these islands. It is the beginning of a journey which we hope you will enjoy as you discover more of Godmanchester's rich and fascinating history.

2

THE FIRST 'HUMANS' IN BRITAIN

The first evidence of 'human' activity in Britain extends backwards up to 950,000 years. This earliest site where worked flint tools have been found is at Happisburgh in Norfolk, the earliest known 'human' settlement in northern Europe. The hominids living in this area of Norfolk walked upright and used tools but had a smaller brain and bigger teeth than us and also had different facial features.

The presence of early hominids in Britain was strongly influenced by the climate. There was great instability with the ebb and flow of ice sheets spreading down from the north. About 450,000 years ago, a severe ice age started and a huge ice cap covered Britain. In one period lasting more than 100,000 years, from 180,000 years ago to 70,000 years ago, there were no people at all in the land we now call Britain and it was completely abandoned. Around 70,000 years ago, 'humans' started to return. These 'humans' were not yet modern people and were commonly known as Neanderthals. Neanderthals were short and stocky, a much better shape for conserving heat. They were very muscular and had distinctive faces, very large noses and a prominent brow ridge. But like our species *homo sapiens*, Neanderthals also buried their dead.

The Arrival of Homo Sapiens

Although 'human' activity began in Britain 950,000 years ago it was not until 45,000 years ago that our species, modern man or *homo sapiens* finally arrived in Europe. *Homo sapiens* evolved in Africa almost 200,000 years ago and about 100,000 years later emerged from Africa.[1] Modern man took another 55,000 years to reach Europe but when they arrived they encountered the Neanderthals. The relationship between modern man and Neanderthals is fascinating and it is likely that DNA evidence will provide further clues in the near future. Neanderthals finally became extinct around 28,000 years ago. The two main factors were competition from modern humans and climate change which forced back trees and reduced the area for hunting.[2] There were now no competing 'human' species and *homo sapiens* reigned supreme. Nevertheless, modern man faced a great challenge for he still had to compete against the elements.

The ice advanced once again and around 20,000 years ago reached its maximum extent known as the last glacial maximum. Ice up to a mile thick covered much of Britain and south of the ice sheet was permafrost, a polar desert with very limited vegetation.[3] The place we now call Godmanchester was probably in the area of permafrost where the earth was frozen to a depth of several meters. Modern humans responded by migrating to mainland Europe. Britain was now inhabited by woolly mammoths. But when the climate changed again and modern man returned to Britain about 15,000 years ago the mammoth faced a major predator. Men hunted mammoths with spears and axes for they were a vital source of food, clothing and shelter. Their huts were often built with mammoth bones and tusks and mammoth hides were stretched over these primitive dwellings. Mammoth bones have been unearthed in many places and local examples can be seen in the Norris Museum at St Ives and at Whittlesey Museum.

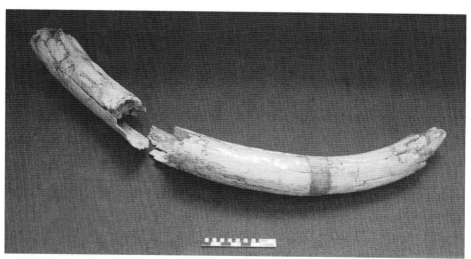

Tusk of mammoth found at Buckden[4] (Norris Museum, St Ives)

Some 13,000 years ago another very cold period returned followed around 11,500 years ago (9500 BC) by the geological period that we continue to live in today. It began as a result of rapid climate change which led to the re-establishment of the Gulf Stream and the return of warm waters to the North Atlantic.[5] It was climate change with a vengeance and rising sea levels gradually separated the British Isles once again from the European mainland. The last remains of the land bridge between Britain and France disappeared.[6] A huge area of land between the English and Danish coasts, now known as Doggerland, disappeared under the North Sea. Our river Great Ouse had formerly wended its way hundreds of miles across Doggerland but now its estuary was at the Wash.[7]

3

GODMANCHESTER'S BEGINNINGS

The new conditions resulting from climate change led to the Mesolithic period, which lasted for five and a half millennia until about 4000 BC. It can be divided into the Early Mesolithic and the Late Mesolithic which began about 7600 BC. The early Mesolithic marks the end of the Old Stone Age (Palaeolithic). The return of forest meant that the characteristic Mesolithic landscape was woodland. The mammoth died out and was replaced by animals whose habitat was that of the forest: red deer, brown bears, wolves, foxes and wild boar. Mesolithic man was adept at hunting these animals and also foraged for plant foods such as berries, fruits and nuts, in particular hazel nuts.[8]

In the Ouse Valley, as the ice retreated it left deposits of alluvium and gravel. Godmanchester lies in the centre of a gravel terrace. The early Mesolithic hunters and gatherers camped adjacent to river terraces and used river valleys as access routes through Huntingdonshire.[9] River valleys including the Ouse Valley were attractive to Mesolithic people because fish, fowl and animals such as deer and pig were both plentiful and vital sources of food. One of the differences between modern humans and the extinct Neanderthals was that modern humans ate fish as well as meat whereas there is no evidence that Neanderthals ate any significant amounts of fish.[10]

Hunter gatherers of the Mesolithic period left archaeological traces in the form of bone and antler work, beads and pendants, stone tools and above all microliths, used as barbs on spears and arrows for hunting. Their simple wooden dwellings have often been inferred from post holes found at sites dated to this period.

Mesolithic mace head from Godmanchester (Norris Museum)

The Neolithic Revolution

One of the greatest changes in the economic history of mankind, known as the 'Neolithic revolution', was the development of settled agriculture. Farming began in the Near East as long as 10,000 years ago but it took about 4,000 years to arrive in Britain. An earlier interpretation believed that the first British farmers came to these islands from Europe during the fifth millennium BC. They generally adopted a kind of slash and burn agriculture as they cleared forest and then moved on to the next area. More recently it has been suggested that the number of incomers was relatively small and that it was largely the indigenous population who adapted to a new way of life.[11] The reasons that the change took place have also been much debated. In many ways farming was much harder than a hunter-gatherer lifestyle. Clearing forest was not only hard work but involved much longer hours of work. The use of the term 'Neolithic revolution' can disguise the fact that the changes did not happen suddenly. Hunting and gathering was still important but farming gradually took over as the main source of food.

Around 4,000 BC the early prehistoric cultivators in the Ouse Valley found that the light soils of the gravel terrace were relatively easy to work. Wheat, unknown in the British Isles in the Mesolithic period, began to be cultivated. The Neolithic period was marked by changes in material culture such as ceramics and polished stone axes. A new flint knapping technology developed and the range of flints uncovered by archaeologists increased very substantially.

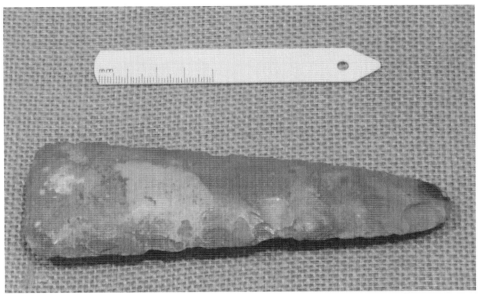

Neolithic flint axehead from Godmanchester (Norris Museum)

Permanent domestic dwellings had their origins in the Neolithic period. For example at nearby Fengate near Peterborough a Neolithic wattle and daub 'house' measuring 7m by 8.5m has been excavated.[12] However, Neolithic peoples in the county still generally lived in temporary dwellings.[13]

Recent archaeological excavations have given us glimpses of the early inhabitants of Godmanchester. A few Neolithic 'monuments' have been found in the county including a mortuary enclosure from the 4th millennium BC in Godmanchester.[14] In 1990, a Neolithic farmstead was discovered and in 1991 English Heritage excavated the five thousand-year-old temple of the sun. The site covers no less than seven hectares and an avenue leading to the temple extends for up to three kilometres. The temple consists of 24 wooden obelisks with pairs of obelisks aligned with major events in the solar and lunar cycles. Furthermore, the temple faces the position on the horizon where the sun rises on two of the prehistoric world's great religious festivals, May Day and Harvest Day.[15]

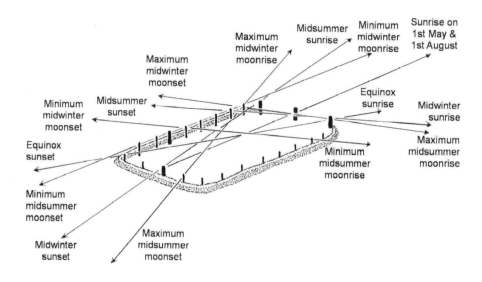

Godmanchester's Neolithic Temple (Bob Burn-Murdoch)

The rituals celebrated at Godmanchester's temple involved slaughtering cattle and possibly human sacrifice. Archaeologists found pieces of ox head and two ox jaw bones at the entrance to the temple and human remains dating from the time when the temple was in use. Although the temple and the avenue leading to the site both only lasted less than a century it remained a place of ritual practice for about a millennium. Subsequently, Bronze Age people dug a series of strange pits on the temple site and filled them with charcoal, twigs, animal bones and flints.

The Bronze Age

The coming of the Early Bronze Age around 2300 BC reflects the technological changes associated with the appearance of metal items. Bronze is an alloy of nine parts copper and one part tin. Gold working appeared in Britain at the same time as bronze and for over a thousand years gold and bronze were the only two metals in use. The Bronze Age can be divided into three periods with the Middle Bronze Age commencing about 1400 BC and the Late Bronze Age lasting from 1100 BC to 800 BC.

The Early Bronze Age is associated with the Beaker people who entered Cambridgeshire from the Wash.[16] The name Beaker comes from their distinctive pottery with inscribed geometric ornamentation found in their burials. These bell-shaped pots were used for drinking and possibly intended for the journey to the afterlife. Houses in the Early Bronze Age were predominantly round with a conical roof and just one entrance. During the Middle Bronze Age the first field systems were introduced and this may reflect increasing population and consequent pressure on the land. Burial practice changed with ashes placed in pottery urns following cremation. In the Late Bronze Age trade with the continent increased. For example in nearby Isleham, Cambridgeshire a hoard of more than 6500 items including swords, axes and knives was found in 1959. Many items in the hoard were imported from the continent.[17]

Bronze Age socketed bronze spearhead from Conington (Norris Museum)

In Godmanchester, Bronze Age people reappear at a burial site in Roman Way. Excavations revealed two cremations and another possible cremation dated from pottery recovered from one of them. Interpretation of these burials remains something of a puzzle. The two positively identified as cremations contained remains of adults. It was not possible for archaeologists to determine whether they were isolated burials or burials located on the edge of a much larger cemetery. The Godmanchester to Huntingdon river crossing was important throughout the Bronze Age and people were drawn to Godmanchester by its geography and its easily worked soil.

The Iron Age

The Iron Age followed the Bronze Age and lasted from about 800BC until the Roman invasion in AD 43. As the name implies, this new epoch was ushered in by further changes in technology particularly in metal working. For example, iron-tipped ploughshares facilitated the cultivation of heavy clay soil.[18] But this was not the only innovation. The potter's wheel and the quern stone, to grind wheat, barley or rye into flour for bread, became widespread. At the end of the period the domestic cat and chicken arrived in Britain. Despite the changes there was much continuity. People continued to live in round wooden huts constructed with wattle and daub. A fireplace in the centre of the single 'room' provided heating and was used for cooking. Iron Age people grew wheat and barley and kept cattle, sheep and pigs. An insight into life in the Iron Age in the Ouse Valley was provided by a reconstruction of an Iron Age farm at Hinchingbrooke Country Park which unfortunately was repeatedly destroyed by acts of vandalism and has now closed. A recent housing development adjacent to Bob's Wood in Hinchingbrooke Country Park is on a hillside location reflecting the Iron Age landscape in the Ouse Valley. The settlement site showed occupation through to the end of the Romano-British period.[19]

A characteristic of the later Iron Age in Britain from about 300 BC onwards was the presence of hill forts such as Maiden Castle and Danebury. Hill forts have variously been interpreted but they had a number of functions. They were ritual centres, market places, food stores and the site of the local chieftain's residence. Huntingdonshire as a low lying county was not natural territory for hill forts. The most common type of settlement in East Anglia was undefended farmsteads. However, a small enclosure built nearby at Stonea was such a 'fort' although there is very little evidence of settlement and it may have been a place for ritual and religious ceremonies. Other local examples include the large circular hill fort at Wandlebury, four miles to the south east of Cambridge and the hill fort at Arbury Camp.

The first century BC witnessed profound social and economic changes in the south and east of the country. There was unprecedented population growth and agriculture improved. Trade with the continent increased and many new 'luxury' goods such as wine-jars arrived. Hill forts gradually disappeared and new settlement types appeared. The changes have been attributed to Belgic tribes who moved into Britain from North West France. They are known for the rich grave goods found with their cremation burials. However, recent interpretations have downplayed the concept of 'invasion' and have suggested that increased trade and contacts with the wider world were responsible for the changes.

The increasing population and agricultural production led to larger scale social organisation.[20] Britain was now controlled by different tribal groups. Huntingdonshire was part of the territory controlled by the Catuvellauni, whose tribal capital was at Verulamium (St Albans).[21] To the east in Essex were the Trinovantes and in the area of Norfolk, the Iceni. The evidence of coinage is important in understanding this period. Names of rulers started to appear on the coins and in the east of England the names were Tasciovanus and Cunobelin. The introduction of dynastic coinage meant that something of major political significance had taken place.[22] Unfortunately our present knowledge is limited. Tasciovanus is known only through the evidence of coins and he became King of the Catuvellauni around 20 BC. The wide distribution of coins bearing his name has been interpreted as a reflection of his increasing power and influence.[23] A coin bearing Tasciovanus' name was found at Sawtry and is now held at the Norris Museum in St Ives.[24] When Tasciovanus died around AD 9 he was succeeded by Cunobelin.[25]

The Coming of the Romans

Julius Caesar's conquest of Gaul had more significance for Britain than his brief forays to these islands in 55 and 54 BC. Roman government had arrived just across the channel and was no longer a distant power. The Romans finally arrived in Britain in AD 43 to claim the prize which they had coveted for decades. The four legions who crossed the channel were II Augusta, IX Hispana, XIV Gemina and XX Valeria Victrix. A legion comprised about 5,000 men but a similar number of archers, light infantry and cavalry supported them. So the total army comprised about 40,000 men. After crossing the channel they arrived at Richborough. The Roman General Plautius defeated the army of the Catuvellauni on the Medway and the new emperor Claudius arrived to lead the army against Colchester.[26] By AD 47 the Romans were in control of the south and east of the country, from the Humber to the Bristol Channel. Godmanchester and the whole of present day Huntingdonshire were now under Roman rule.

The Romans organised their areas of local government in accordance with the previous tribal organisation. Several tribal rulers were granted the status of a client king. One of these client kings was Prasutagus, ruler of a wealthy area of East Anglia occupied by the Iceni tribe. When Prasutagus died he left half of his estate to Nero and half to his two daughters. However, the Romans assumed control of the area, publically flogged his Queen Boudicca and raped her two young daughters. The response was ferocious. Boudicca was joined by the Trinovantes from Essex whose grievances against Roman rule were that their farms and houses had been confiscated and given to veteran soldiers at Colchester. The popular picture of Boudicca as a tall red-headed woman with a harsh voice and dressed in tunic with a gold torque around her neck is painted by Dio Cassius.[27] But the Roman historian Dio Cassius wrote about a century and a half after Boudicca's rebellion and to some extent his account reflects the threats to Roman rule in his own day.

The challenge posed by the rebellion was very real and had it succeeded could have brought an end to Roman occupation in Britain. Boudicca led her army on a rampage of destruction. Colchester, London, St Albans and Chelmsford were engulfed in flames and thousands killed. The Ninth Legion commanded by Quintus Petillius Cerialis, unsuccessfully attempted to relieve Colchester and many men were killed. The Roman governor of Britain Suetonius Paullinus was in Anglesey and could do little to save London from its fate. His response to the crisis was immediate and Paullinus marched southward with his troops. The Boudiccan hordes might have been successful at guerrilla warfare but attempting to take on the Roman army in a final pitched battle was suicidal. How Boudicca died is disputed but it was the end of this primeval Battle of Britain. Roman ascendancy was now firmly established.

Godmanchester witnessed the response to the rebellion for the Ninth Legion would probably have passed through Godmanchester on the Roman road to Colchester. Michael Green found evidence of major fires in Godmanchester which he dated to the period of Boudicca's uprising. However, whether this evidence has anything to do with Boudicca's rebellion is doubtful. Interpreting archaeological evidence is not always straightforward. Fires are not always started deliberately and as today happen by accident. The archaeologist is faced with the near impossible task of differentiating between evidence of Boudicca's revolt and the results of a bakery fire.[28]

The Roman presence had first arrived in Godmanchester when an auxiliary fort was established within a year of the invasion of England by Claudius in AD 43. The fort was soon dismantled as the frontier moved northwards. Following Boudicca's revolt, a second fort was established during the rule of Nero (54-68). The civilian settlement remained and during the Flavian period (69-98) the town centre was replanned and plots were laid out adjoining Ermine Street. One interpretation for the way that land was allotted such as along Ermine Street suggested that settlers were given land in return for providing accommodation for official travellers in their own homes.[29]

Godmanchester (*Durovigutum*[30]) controlled the river crossing of Ermine Street, the military highway from *Londinium* (London) to *Lindum* (Lincoln) and *Eburacum* (York) and the east to west road from *Durolipons* (Cambridge) known as the *Via Devana*. Ermine Street ran north from Royston (along what is now the A1198) and as it reached Godmanchester it was located fractionally to the east of London Road, entering the town through the South Gate. The road widens to form a market place in the middle of the town. After exiting through the North Gate in Cambridge Street, it crossed Chadley Lane close to the west side of the church and continued east of Post Street before crossing Post Street and heading towards the river crossing. An old road can still be detected which allegedly heads towards the fording point of the river to the west of the medieval Bridge.

Whether the actual crossing was by means of a bridge, a raised causeway under the water or a fording point in shallow water has not been conclusively determined.

Masonry from Godmanchester's North Gate (Norris Museum, St Ives).[31]

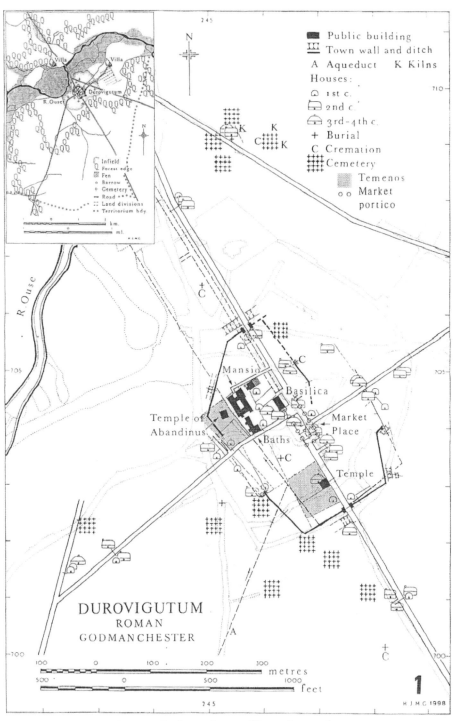

Roman Godmanchester (Durovigutum)

The main archaeological excavations of Godmanchester were carried out by Michael Green over a period of 25 years starting in 1951. Much of our knowledge about Roman Godmanchester is derived from Michael Green's excavations. However, when the Rev Professor William Frend died in 2005 his obituary in the Daily Telegraph referred to a royal contribution to the excavations. Professor Frend, Fellow of Gonville and Caius College Cambridge, 'used to take Prince Charles and other undergraduates out on Sunday afternoons to dig a Roman site' in Godmanchester.[32]

During the early years of the second century, a *mansio* or inn and baths were built at Godmanchester. Godmanchester's *mansio* now provided overnight accommodation and fresh horses for official travellers. Subsequently the *mansio* became a tax collection centre. At over a hundred meters long the building was very large by contemporary standards. Excavations led by Michael Green uncovered two stable blocks each holding six or more horses or mules. *Mansios* were located about a day's journey apart at staging posts on Roman roads. For example, the *mansio* uncovered in 2006 at Alfoldean, West Sussex was located at the strategically important crossing of Stane Street and the river Arun on the road from Chichester to London.[33]

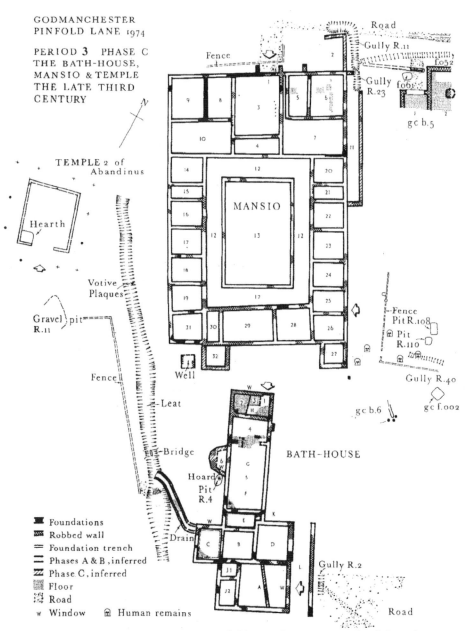

GODMANCHESTER
PINFOLD LANE 1974

PERIOD **3** PHASE C
THE BATH-HOUSE,
MANSIO & TEMPLE
THE LATE THIRD
CENTURY

TEMPLE 2 of
Abandinus

Hearth

Votive
Plaques

Gravel pit
R.11

Fence

Well

Leat

Bridge

Hoard
Pit
R.4

Drain

Road

Gully R.11

Gully foot

Gully
R.23

gc b.5

Fence 2

MANSIO

Fence
Pit R.108

Pit
R.110

Gully R.40

gc f.002

gc b.6

BATH-HOUSE

Gully R.2

Road

Road

Foundations
Robbed wall
Foundation trench
Phases A & B, inferred
Phase C, inferred
Floor
Road
w Window   ⌂ Human remains

Mansio (inn) and Bath House Pinfold Lane (Courtesy Michael Green)

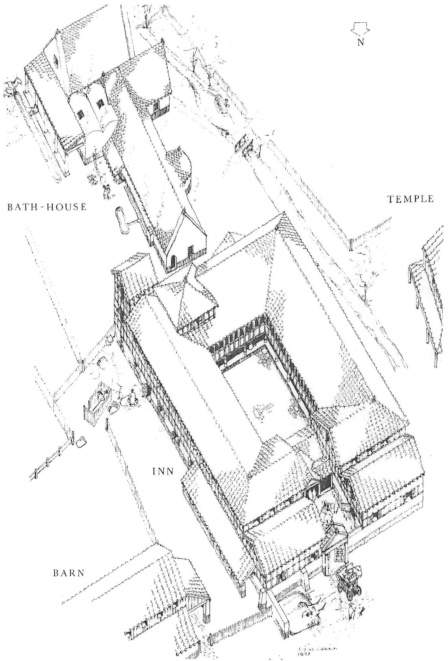

N

BATH-HOUSE

TEMPLE

INN

BARN

Reconstruction of Mansio and Baths by Michael Green

In the first years of the third century a basilica or town hall consisting of six bays was built in the centre of the town. The presence of a basilica may indicate that Godmanchester had achieved the formal status of a *vicus* with a legal constitution and rights of self-government.[34] The original walls of the town were wooden and it had four gates. By the late third century Godmanchester had stone walls three meters thick and gateways. The South Gate, on the site of Roman Gate Flats at the junction of London Street and London Road, was very large with two gate towers flanking the 30 foot wide Ermine Street.[35]

Roman Gate flats on the site of the South Gate

The building of the wall was severely hampered by a major fire in 296 which badly damaged the inn and the bathhouse. The inn was not occupied again until the middle of the fourth century.[36] The current roads, The Causeway, Old Court Hall, London Street, Earning Street and Cambridge Street roughly follow the Roman Wall.

The size and importance of Godmanchester during the Roman period remains a matter of debate. John Wacher and Guy de la Bedoyere regarded Godmanchester as a minor town.[37] Neil Faulkner suggested that around AD 100 Godmanchester must have been a 'scruffy roadside hamlet'.[38] However, communities change over time and the building of the *mansio* and baths was a significant development. Tim Malim paints a picture of Godmanchester being a busy market town in the second century. As well as agricultural activity there is evidence of pottery production, metalworking, bone-working, baking, dairy processing and beer making. Although a considerable amount of pottery was imported from the continent an indigenous pottery industry to provide for the needs of the army and local people was established very early in the Roman period.[39] Michael Green found extensive evidence of dairy production in Godmanchester including an early second-century cheese press. The dairy industry was largely based on sheep rather than cattle. Excavations also uncovered amphoræ containing mackerel or fish paste and evidence of shops selling glass and Samian ware.[40]

Samian ware dish from Godmanchester (Norris Museum, St Ives)

By the close of the second century, the walls of Godmanchester enclosed a town of some 20 acres. However, the town may have contracted in the third century as a result of flooding reducing the surrounding areas available for agriculture.[41]

Remains of Roman Godmanchester in a garden in Pipers Lane

Throughout Godmanchester's history, its people have lived in a wide range of buildings. In the earlier Roman period many would have lived in traditional timber-framed round huts. Villas were only for the very affluent. Neil Faulkner has mapped the distribution of known villas and most are concentrated in the Romanised south eastern part of England.[42] One of these villas was found at Rectory Farm to the north east of the town. The villa was a corridor house with a cobbled forecourt and garden. It had two large-aisled barns and four other large buildings with wide stone wall foundations and 32 ovens.[43] Michael Green identified a barn for corn and crewyards for cattle. Attempts have recently been made to reconstruct the gardens of Romano British houses. The garden at Rectory Farm villa had an ornamental pond.[44] Examination of macrofossils found at the site identified spruce, box, yew, grape, beet, marigold, fig, fennel and opium poppy. Prior to this discovery, spruce was thought to be a post-medieval introduction.[45]

Roman burials have been uncovered in Godmanchester for over a century. In 1905, 8 urned cremations were found at Green End and in 1990, 55 urned cremations were found at Rectory Farm.[46] In 1991 a fascinating cremation was discovered accidentally in Pinfold Lane when foundations of a garage were being dug. The cremation remains had been placed in a Samian vase flanked by figurines of a horse and a bull. Corinne Duhig identified the bone fragments as belonging to a child of around seven or eight years old. Interpretation of these rare figurines has aroused controversy. The figures may have been toys or at least ornaments suitable for children. Alternatively they may have been sacrificial offerings to the gods, possibly as a substitute for live animals which the bereaved family may not have been able to afford.[47] This burial was permitted within the town because the deceased was a young child.

Horse and bull figurines from Pinfold Lane

Inhumation burial was adopted in Godmanchester during the third century. Cemeteries were established outside the town walls and along the approach roads to Godmanchester. A dozen cemeteries have now been uncovered outside the Roman town.[48] A series of skeletons were found in 1982 during the building of Porch Close.

Roman skeletons excavated in Porch Close 1982 (courtesy Graham Reynolds)

An excavation at The Parks in 1998 uncovered a cemetery containing 62 largely well-preserved individuals which probably dated to the fourth century AD. Most of the people were buried without grave goods but 13 burials were accompanied by coins, bracelets, finger rings and earrings.[49] At least five individuals were decapitated with the head placed at the feet.[50] Decapitation is variously interpreted from being a ritual killing to religious belief locating the head as the seat of the soul. In the latter interpretation, decapitation would prevent the dead from walking, haunting or disturbing the living.[51]

4

FROM THE EARLY MEDIEVAL PERIOD TO THE CHARTERS

The Anglo-Saxons

The period following the end of Roman dominance in England used to be popularly known as the 'Dark Ages'. Any historical writing about this period must be tentative because our knowledge is still limited. However new archaeological discoveries are making the period considerably less 'dark' than it used to be. The term 'Dark Ages' was not a complimentary term and was used not just to suggest ignorance of the period but to imply that it was a time of cultural poverty. The discoveries that have been made in the recent past have also undermined this idea and shown that the craftsmanship of much that has been unearthed is of a high order. A more appropriate term, the early medieval period, is now commonly used. The early medieval period covered several centuries during which enormous changes took place. The small kingdoms of the early Anglo-Saxons had become England by the end of the period. The Anglo-Saxons brought pagan beliefs with them but by the time of the Norman Conquest, England was a Christian nation.

The coming of the Anglo-Saxons is an area of continuing controversy among historians and archaeologists. There are debates over the number of Anglo-Saxons who came, their social make up and the extent to which the end of Roman Britain was a major break with the past. Whether the Anglo-Saxons were conquerors or settlers is also a matter of dispute. This is not the place to examine these questions in detail. However, there is increasing archaeological evidence that the end of Roman Rule did not result in a collapse of society. There was continuity as well as change. Furthermore, it can at least be said that there is no evidence of widespread slaughter of the Romano-British local populations. Therefore the coming of the Anglo-Saxons is now more commonly interpreted as a migration rather than invasion and conquest.[52] The years 450-600 are frequently referred to by archaeologists as the 'Migration Period'.

The term 'Anglo-Saxon' includes various groups of Germanic peoples who came from territories that we now call Denmark, the Netherlands and Germany. Among the various ethnic groups, the Angles settled in the east of the country. Godmanchester was only a small hamlet in this period. The Ouse Valley was occupied by the Middle Angles in the western part of the Angles' territory. Their settlements predominated in river terraces where the light soils could be easily ploughed. Evidence of their presence survives in pottery remains found in Godmanchester and also in place names.[53]

Any possible claim for independence by the Middle Angles was short lived and Godmanchester and the surrounding area came under the control of Mercia during the late sixth or early seventh century. The Kingdom of Mercia covered the territory we now call the Midlands but began to rapidly expand its power at this time. Within a few decades it became the most powerful of the Saxon kingdoms in England. Mercia's principal centres were at Lichfield, Tamworth and Repton.[54]

The social structure of the Middle Saxon period (650-850) comprised *thegns*, (pronounced thanes) *cnichts*, (or knights) *coerls* (pronounced carls) and serfs. The thegn received his land as a grant from the king which comprised at least five hides (600 acres). *Thegns, cnichts,* and *coerls* were all obliged to serve the King in times of war. *Coerls* were the head of free peasant households. Serfs were not freemen but tenants of landlords for life. The main cereal crop in the early Anglo-Saxon period was barley but wheat gradually became more common. Cereals were used to make bread, beer and pottage. The Anglo-Saxon loaf was small and round and was baked on hearth stones in most households. King Alfred's fabled 'cakes' would probably have been these small loaves.[55]

Anglo-Saxon buildings were made of wood and archaeologists have been able to identify them by discolouration in the soil revealing the position of post holes. One of their characteristic buildings was the *Grubenhaus*, examples of which have been found in Godmanchester. The word *Grubenhaus* from the German means literally a pit house and was a sunken-floor building. Objects linked with the production of textiles are frequently found in *Grubenhaus* buildings suggesting that weaving was one of the activities practised in them. In the Anglo-Saxon period, these *Gruben-haus* buildings were frequently grouped together in clusters within an enclosure to form a small hamlet or village. A visit to West Stow Anglo-Saxon village in Suffolk gives a clearer picture of the kind of buildings used by these peoples.

Until relatively recently, archaeologists and historians believed that England was an economic backwater during the Middle Saxon period. However, archaeological excavations at Southampton and elsewhere have revealed a very different picture of rapidly expanding trade.[56] A good example of commonly traded goods was Ipswich ware pottery. Ipswich ware has been found in Godmanchester and at sites throughout England, as far north as York and as far south as Kent. Chemical analysis has shown that all the Ipswich Ware excavated in England to date was made from clay from the Ipswich area.[57] Ipswich was a major centre of trade in the Middle Saxon period as were other large communities known as *Wics*: London (*Lunden-wic*) and Southampton (*Hamwic*).

The discoveries at Sutton Hoo have done much to illuminate the early history of East Anglia but relatively little was known about Mercia until a dramatic discovery by Terry Herbert using a metal detector in Staffordshire in 2009. The Staffordshire hoard consisting of more than 1500 pieces represent the largest find of Anglo-Saxon gold ever discovered. The finds comprise mainly weaponry but also three Christian objects which have been dated to the seventh century. The Christian items were a pendant cross, a decorated gold processional cross and an object with a biblical text which may also have been a processional cross. The text contains the phrase 'Rise up O Lord and may thy enemies be dispersed'. The finds may help to shed light on Anglo-Saxon Society and the relationship between paganism and Christianity.

The large number of weapons in the Staffordshire hoard reinforces the idea of the seventh century as a warlike society led by a military aristocracy. The two Mercian processional crosses found in Staffordshire may have been carried into battle in the belief that the new Christian God may give the king victory over his enemies.[58] The conversion of England to Christianity was not straightforward. Some early kings worshipped both Christ and Woden whereas others reverted to paganism after adopting Christianity. History is usually written by the winners and we should beware of falling into the trap of believing that the triumph of Christianity was an assured outcome.

On a far less dramatic scale, other archaeological finds have added to our knowledge of life in Godmanchester during these centuries. On 2 June 1999, *The Hunts Post* reported news of a rare discovery of Saxon remains on a site adjacent to the Total garage on the A1198. The excavation, carried out by the Hertfordshire Archaeological Trust, found six Saxon buildings and an assortment of domestic appliances including pots, loom weights bone pins and evidence of textile production.[59] The finds dated from the 5th to the 8th centuries and Hertfordshire Archaeological Trust suggested that about 30 people lived on the site. Domestic buildings both *Grubenhäuser* and timber-framed were uncovered during the excavation.

Silver was used for several purposes including jewellery. In September 2003 while using a metal-detector, Mr S Ashford found a silver object in Godmanchester dating approximately from the early 6th century. The object is circular with a loop at the top and still has five of the original seven projecting lobes. It measures 34 mm from top to bottom (including the loop) and weighs 6.37g. The item is unusual and may be one half of a clasp or a pendant. It has a scrolled swastika motif, often found on jewellery from southwest Scandinavia and Anglo-Saxon England in this period. For example, a similar swastika motif appears on a pair of silver-gilt brooches of the early 6th century from nearby Barrington, Cambridgeshire. Grants from the Town Council, the Community Association and Huntingdonshire Local History Society enabled the Porch Museum to acquire this rare find and it now takes pride of place in the museum.

Early medieval **silver clasp or pendant (Porch Museum)**

The Coming of the Danes

In the ninth century a new threat appeared. The term often used to describe the people who provided this threat is 'Vikings'. But 'Viking' is not an ethnic term but an activity or occupation, largely restricted to young adult males. *Fara i viking* meant to go on a Viking expedition which involved raiding and also trading. Contemporaries did not use the term, 'Vikings' but Norsemen, Danes and heathen. For example, *The Anglo-Saxon Chronicle* records that in 865/6 'a great heathen force came into English land and took winter quarters in East Anglia'. The 'force' went on to conquer Northumbria and York and then back to East Anglia.

In 869, the East Anglian King Edmund was defeated in battle and killed by the 'heathen force'. Edmund was buried at Beadoriceworth, (now Bury St Edmunds) and venerated as a saint and martyr. Pilgrimage to his shrine brought great wealth to the church. Guthrum was part of that 'great heathen force' and by the latter half of the 9th century, Guthrum had become the Danish king of the area known as the Danelaw, which included parts of the kingdoms of Mercia and Northumbria. Guthrum made substantial inroads into Wessex before he was finally halted by Alfred at the Battle of Edington in 878.

After the conquest of East Anglia, Huntingdon was an important seat of the Danes. The Danes built a '*burh*' (a defensive stronghold) on the high ground but its precise location is disputed. A community excavation of Mill Common, Huntingdon formed part of the celebrations for the 800th anniversary of Huntingdon's charter in 2005. The excavation was led by Richard Mortimer and he believes that the most likely identification is the Castle site, close to the point where Ermine Street crossed the river.[60] Danish origin of the shire is borne out by an entry in *The Anglo-Saxon Chronicle* referring to Huntingdon as a military centre to which the surrounding district owed allegiance. Between 865 and 879 Godmanchester was raided by Danish Armies and occupied by Guthrum after 879. Huntingdonshire, Cambridgeshire and a large part of Bedfordshire all came under Danish rule.

The Danish presence in the area known as the Danelaw is difficult to detect in the archaeological record. There are remarkably few grave goods and artefacts but the language reflects Danish words such as egg, dirt, fellow, ill, leg and sky. There are also place names such as villages with the suffix 'by' or 'thorpe', meaning farmstead or hamlet. In Huntingdonshire, Ellington Thorpe and Toseland have names of Danish origin. One possible interpretation of the name Godmanchester is that 'Godman' refers to the Danish ruler Guthrum. In Godmanchester, there is no evidence of Danish activity detected to date. The archaeologist Dawn Hadley suggested that the reason is that the Danes rapidly became 'settlers' and went out of their way to live in peace with their new Saxon neighbours and adopt their way of life.[61] After 879, Guthrum ruled East Anglia according to local custom rather than alien Danish ones. For example, Guthrum adopted Christianity and minted coins, a practice unknown in his homeland.

Kings of Wessex re-conquered what became the English nation. It began under the reign of Alfred but the surviving sources for Alfred's reign are particularly biased.[62] Alfred is portrayed in these sources as a larger than life hero, no less than Alfred 'the Great'. In the nineteenth century Alfred became a cult figure, 'the most perfect character in history' and 'the favourite story in English nurseries'.[63] However, more recent historians have shown that Alfred had feet of clay like the rest of us.[64] Nevertheless, politically his reign was of great significance. Although Wessex had taken over from Mercia as the dominant Saxon kingdom before Alfred was born, Alfred began the process that transformed Wessex into England.

Alfred's son, Edward the Elder (reigned 899-924) drove the Danes out of Godmanchester and Huntingdon. Athelstan 'the Glorious', Alfred's grandson, (reigned 924-39) extended the rule of Wessex to nearly all of England. By the tenth century, England had finally emerged. Queen Elizabeth II celebrated the 1,000 year anniversary of the English monarchy in 1973. This millennium was based on the coronation of King Edgar in Bath Abbey in May 973. However, the 're-conquest' of England was not the end of the Danes. In 1009 'an immense raiding army' led by Thorkell 'the Tall' arrived. *The Anglo-Saxon Chronicle* records that Huntingdonshire was overrun by the Vikings in 1010 who 'ravaged and burnt the land and even went into the wild fens where they slew men and cattle'. In 1013, the wonderfully named Swein Forkbeard arrived in Sandwich and 'went very quickly about East Anglia…and upward along the Trent until he came to Gainsborough'. King Ethelred fled to Normandy and Swein became King of England. Swein's son Cnut succeeded to the throne followed by his grandsons Harold Harefoot and Harthacanute, who ruled England until 1042. On the death of Harthacanute, the House of Wessex was restored in the form of Edward the Confessor.

The term Huntingdonshire was not used until the year 1011 when *The Anglo-Saxon Chronicle* recorded that a Danish army had 'overrun' half of the county. Huntingdonshire like other counties was divided into four administrative units called 'hundreds'. The organisation of these hundreds probably dates from the tenth century. Huntingdonshire had four: Norman Cross, Hurstingstone, Toseland and Leightonstone. The hundred courts met regularly to settle disputes and enforce law and order. These meeting places were often in remote areas marked by a stone or a tree. Three of these stones still survive and the stone of Hurstingstone can now be seen in the grounds of the Norris Museum in St Ives. Godmanchester was in the hundred of Toseland.

Hurstingstone

The events of more than a thousand years ago still leave their mark on the landscape of Godmanchester. When Edward the Elder recaptured Godmanchester in 917 he refortified it. The old Roman road through the town (Ermine Street) was abandoned and the current road system around the Roman wall was laid out.[65]

The three watermill sites are also a reminder of the Danes in Godmanchester. Mechanically powered mills could use very large stones of more than two meters in diameter whereas hand querns were very small. Mills therefore provided a much more efficient way of grinding corn into flour than using a hand-operated quern. The Mill Lade, which leads from the Great Ouse close to the lock down to the Causeway, was excavated by hand under Danish direction. The workers used wattle hurdles daubed with mud to keep back the waters and wicker baskets to carry away the spoil.[66]

The Mill Lade

Domesday Book

When William conquered England in 1066 the whole country came under his personal ownership. The king granted most of that land to 'Norman' lords, although strictly speaking not all of them came from Normandy. The king retained for himself land which represented about one sixth of the landed revenues of the country.[67] Under William, about 200 Norman barons held land as 'tenants-in-chief' from the Crown. In return tenants-in-chief were required to provide the king with military manpower. The use of the term tenant was important because nobody was above having their lands taken away by the king if they were disloyal.

A threat of military invasion by the Danes triggered the compilation of what became known as the 'Domesday Book'. While William the Conqueror was holding his court in Gloucester in the winter of 1085, he determined to establish how the country 'was occupied'. William sent his men all over England to find out who held the land and how many hides of land there were in each shire. A hide was the area of land that a team of eight oxen could plough in a year, roughly 120 acres. A hide was also the unit of land upon which taxation was based in Anglo-Saxon society. Much ink has been shed by historians seeking to interpret the figures recorded in Domesday but Huntingdonshire had somewhere around 800 hides.[68]

Domesday Book is a unique record of feudal England in 1086. *The Anglo-Saxon Chronicle* proudly records how 'not an ox, a cow, a pig was left out that was not set in his document'. Two volumes were produced. The first covered Essex, Suffolk and Norfolk and the second covered the rest of the country with the exception of the northernmost counties. Domesday represents a complete inventory of landholdings in the country, by county, by hundred and by manor.

The essential unit of local government was the manor. The manorial system was well developed before 1066 but following the Conquest the Saxon manorial lords were replaced by Normans. Under Norman rule there was no land without a lord of the manor. Typically a manor comprised the lord's own lands, known as *demesne* (pronounced demean) land and other land allocated to dependent peasants. In return peasants had to pay rent to the lord in cash and kind and also work for the lord on his *demesne* land. The lord of the manor usually appointed a reeve to organise the farming of the *demesne* land. Working on the lord's land could involve a substantial number of days a year and therefore jeopardise the productivity of the peasant's own land particularly at harvest time. All tenants whether free or unfree had to attend the manor court and swear allegiance to their lord.

The lord controlled everything: rents, access to land and even marriage. For example when a tenant's son or daughter got married, the tenant had to make a payment known as a merchet to the lord. If the daughter was found guilty of fornication or got pregnant outside of marriage a payment called a leyrwite was made. When the tenant died the heir had to pay a heriot, a kind of death duty. Originally this comprised the best beast but this was later changed to a money payment. Payment of heriots was only abolished in 1922. The lord also controlled justice through the manor court. Local disputes such as failure to pay debts or a tenant's animal destroying another tenant's crops were settled in the manor court. The resulting fees called amercements went to the lord of the manor. Mills were also a visible symbol of manorial power. The lord of the manor invested in mills and recouped his investment by compelling his tenants to use it.

Only about 14 per cent of the English population was 'free' at the time of the Domesday Book in 1086.[69] Although most of the rural population of England were 'unfree' they did not all share the same economic circumstances. Villeins generally rented farms of about thirty acres, considerably larger than the land occupied by bordars who were smallholders. However, even relatively prosperous villeins were still unfree in that they had no appeal to a royal court if their lord abused their rights. Those who were unfree could only appeal to the manorial court.

The manor of Godmanchester was Crown land, held by Edward the Confessor prior to the Conquest and after 1086 by William. It comprised 14 hides (about 1680 acres) valued at £40. To put this in perspective, an 'average' village was about five hides.[70] Like most Huntingdonshire parishes, Godmanchester had no freemen or sokemen but only villeins and bordars. Godmanchester had many more (80) of the more prosperous villeins than bordars who numbered 16. Domesday also records no less than 6,000 mills in the country and the three watermill sites built during the Danish period in Godmanchester are recorded among them. Finally, Domesday records that there was a priest and a church in Godmanchester.

In 1190, Richard I granted the manor of Godmanchester to the Earl of Huntingdon, at the increased sum of £50. David, Earl of Huntingdon (1144-1219) had impressive grandparents. On his paternal side his grandfather was David I King of Scotland and William de Warenne, the Earl of Surrey on his mother's side. The Earl of Huntingdon still held Godmanchester from the king in 1212 by the service of a knight's fee. A knight's fee was the requirement to provide a fully armed and equipped knight and his retainers to the king for forty days each year. The obligation of knight's fees was often met by a money payment.

The Charters of Godmanchester

The year 1212 was a momentous year in the history of Godmanchester. Under the charter of 1212 King John granted the manor to 'the men of Godmanchester' to hold at the fee-farm rent of £120 a year. The annual rent was payable to the Crown. Godmanchester became a self-governing manor and the people of Godmanchester now had the status of 'Free Tenants'.

An understanding of the reign of King John, one of the most crucial periods in English history, can help to put the Godmanchester charter in context. As the fourth legitimate son of Henry II, John was not expected to become king. But when Richard I (known as the Lionheart) died from gangrene in 1199, John became King of England. John also acquired a major part of what is now France. These possessions comprised almost all the Western half of France from Normandy, through Maine and Anjou to Aquitaine and Gascony in the south. However, John found it difficult to hang on to these lands for the Normans were no longer prepared to support Angevin rule. They switched their loyalty to Philip, King of France who set out to acquire them by force.

The crucial loss was the 'impregnable' fortress of Chateau Gaillard. John's lands quickly succumbed until finally the great prize of Rouen fell in June 1204. The death of John's mother, Queen Eleanor of Aquitaine, in April 1204 had removed any legal obstacle to further progress by Philip and Poitou was the next to fall. The loss of Normandy and Anjou in 1204 was a major crisis for King John. Plans put into action to recover the lost territory were delayed by the barons' recalcitrance and their lack of enthusiasm for the campaign. An expedition in 1206 was moderately successful and at least stabilised John's lands in the south. A direct result of the exposure of the English Channel following the loss of Normandy was the birth of the Royal Navy at Portsmouth.

Huge amounts of money were raised in building up a massive war chest for regaining John's territory. As we have seen in return for grants of land, 'tenants-in-chief' had to provide the king with knights for military service. They also had the alternative of making a money payment known as 'scutage' instead. Mercenaries could then be purchased with the money. John raised the rate for 'scutage' from one mark to two and then to three marks by 1213. No less than seven 'scutage' taxes were raised between 1199 and 1206 but the imposition of wealth taxes achieved many times the yield from 'scutage'. More than £60,000 was raised from a wealth tax in 1207. It was known as 'the Thirteenth Tax' because the rate was 12*d* for every mark (13*s* 4*d*).[71] The tax was assessed on the rents and moveable wealth from 'every laymen throughout England'.[72] During his dispute with the Pope over the appointment of a new Archbishop of Canterbury, John managed to extract large sums from church estates. Various ways of raising money were deployed and one of them was granting charters. Many towns and villages received their charter at this period including Huntingdon in 1205, Stafford 1206, Liverpool 1207 and Great Yarmouth 1208. In 1211 the Crown's income was six times that at the beginning of John's reign.[73]

In 1212, the year of Godmanchester's charter, John planned his return to France. Major preparations were underway and the necessary provisions were sent to Portsmouth. Records of those required for military service on the basis of their landholdings were updated and knights were summoned to Poitou. But a Welsh revolt changed the king's mind and he redirected his attention to Wales.[74] Thus the opening words of Godmanchester's charter where John introduced himself as King of England, Duke of Normandy and Earl of Anjou had little reality on the ground. Nevertheless, these titles continued to be used in many charters issued by John including Magna Carta in 1215. Two years after Godmanchester's charter King John set out to recover his French possessions. The campaign of 1214 failed and two years later John was dead as a result of dysentery contracted at Lynn. The loss of Normandy and Anjou in 1204 turned out to be more than a major crisis for King John. It was the end of the Angevin empire and a major turning point in European history. The French Capetian Kings now dominated Western Europe and the Anglo-Norman state was at an end. In 1259 under the Treaty of Paris, John's son Henry III gave up his claims to Normandy and Anjou.[75]

In 1897, Mr C Mayfield the Borough Surveyor gave a lecture on the history of Godmanchester in St Mary's parish room. He commented that King John's charter for Godmanchester represented just 168 words and was 'a very small and insignificant document…to look at not much larger than a man's hand'.

King John's Charter 1212
(Reproduced by permission of Huntingdonshire Archives)

The text of the charter reads as follows:

John, by the Grace of God, King of England, Duke of Normandy and Aquitaine Earl of Anjou-to Archbishops, Bishops, Abbots, Earls, Barons, Judiciaries, Viscounts, Sheriffs and Bailiffs and all his faithful subjects- Greeting. Know ye that we have granted and by this our Charter have confirmed to our Men of Godmanchester, our Manor of Gumcestr to be held of us and our heirs at Fee Farm, together with all things belonging to the Farm of that Manor for £120 per annum weight and number- To witness moiety at the feast of St Michael and the other moiety at Easter at our Treasury. Therefore we will and firmly command that our aforesaid men of Godmanchester have and hold of us and our heirs the aforesaid Manor of Gumcester truly and in peace, freely, quietly and surely with all privileges belonging to the Farm of the said Manor at the aforesaid yearly farm of £120 so long as they shall well and truly pay to us the aforesaid Farm Rent.

Godmanchester's charter resulted in a considerable increase in income for the king. Under the terms of the charter, £120 had to be paid each year to the king, a substantial increase on the £50 paid when David, Earl of Huntingdon held the manor. According to the wording of the charter, half (moiety) was to be paid at the feast of St Michael (29 September) and the other half at Easter. The £120 paid to the Crown had to be collected from property holders in the town, both resident and non-resident. This resulted in considerable work for the town's bailiffs who had to maintain lists of properties on which the tax was based. The administration of Godman-chester was the responsibility of two bailiffs chosen by the inhabitants of the town and appointed annually. They controlled the entry of outsiders to the town, administered conveyance of property and rents to be paid. The earliest recorded meeting place of the court was the hall of the Prior of Merton, located just to the east of St Mary's Parish Church. The two bailiffs at this meeting on 14 March 1280 were William Clerk and Reginald, son of Robert.[76]

The other important charter in Godmanchester's history was granted by King James I in 1604. Just before her death on 24 March 1603 Elizabeth I indicated that James VI of Scotland should succeed her. The Privy Council proclaimed the Scottish King James to be James I of England. James I took more than a month to travel from Edinburgh to London and his journey took him through Newcastle, York, Doncaster and Newark until he arrived at Hinchingbrooke House at the end of April. Here he was entertained by Sir Oliver Cromwell (1563-1655), the future Lord Protector's Uncle. On April 29th James passed through Godmanchester and he was received on the boundaries by a procession of nine score (180) ploughs. James contin-ued his journey to Royston and he finally arrived in London on 11 May 1603.

The following year 1604, Godmanchester was incorporated as a free borough and granted a horse and cattle fair under the charter of King James I.[77] The Corporation was formed with 2 bailiffs and 12 assistants. The 'free tenants of Godmanchester' became burgesses and a Town Clerk was appointed. One of the first bye laws was to attach the rights of common to the house as well as the individual. The two bailiffs for 1683, Thomas

Betts and John Wright, are immortalised on the wall next to the entrance to the Queen Elizabeth School.

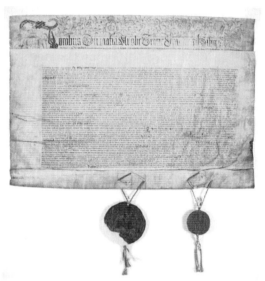

King James' Charter 1604
(Reproduced by permission of Huntingdonshire Archives)

Godmanchester's bailiffs in 1683

The 400th Anniversary of James' visit to Godmanchester on 29 April 2003 was commemorated by a visit of His Royal Highness, The Duke of Gloucester accompanied by the Vice Lord-Lieutenant of Cambridgeshire,

Mr Michael Marshall. The Duke of Gloucester was welcomed by the Mayor, Anne Looker.

Godmanchester Mayor, Anne Looker welcomes H.R.H. Duke of Gloucester

In 1835, a mayor, 4 Alderman and 12 Councillors were established under the Municipal Corporations Act. In 1961 Godmanchester lost its status as a borough when it united with Huntingdon to become the borough of Huntingdon and Godmanchester governed by a Mayor, 6 Aldermen and 18 Councillors. Twenty one years later on 1 April 1982, Godmanchester Town Council was established and Janet McCartney was elected mayor. The Godmanchester mayoral chain which had been presented to the Corporation of Godmanchester in commemoration of Queen Victoria's Jubilee in 1897 returned to Godmanchester. The chain is made from 18 carat gold and one of the medallions contains the dates of the charters, although the first is given the date of 1213.

5

WHO WERE THE PEOPLE?

Population

Attempts to calculate the population of Godmanchester over its history are fraught with problems. However, attempts at establishing broad trends in population movements can be made. Population estimates for early periods are particularly precarious. Michael Green suggested a Godmanchester population of around 200 in the Roman period. The basis of his estimate was the corn yield from the arable town lands.[78] By contrast, a reconstruction of Roman Godmanchester in the Norris Museum, St Ives estimates Godmanchester's population at between 400 and 500 in AD 290.

It is commonly believed that the population of England fell significantly between the end of the Roman period and the seventh century. For example, Stocker suggests that the population may have fallen below a million, fewer than in the Iron Age.[79] The causes of the population decrease are unknown but there are some plausible suggestions. The most likely is disease. Plague was endemic in the early medieval period. There were major outbreaks of epidemic disease in England in the seventh century particularly in the years AD 664-6 and again in 684-7. It has been suggested that these outbreaks may have been as devastating as the Black Death in the fourteenth century.[80] Evidence for these 'plagues' is documentary (*The Anglo-Saxon Chronicle* and Bede) rather than based on examination of physical remains. *The Anglo-Saxon Chronicle* records that in 664, 'there was much pestilence on the island of Britain' and Bede writes, 'in the same year, (i.e. 664) a sudden pestilence also depopulated the southern coasts of Britain and afterwards extending into the province of the Northumbrians, ravaged the country far and near, and destroyed a great multitude of men'.[81] The nature of these epidemics is therefore not without controversy. We have no knowledge of the impact of epidemic disease on Godmanchester. But disease patterns of the seventh century were quite different to those of today.

For example, leprosy and tuberculosis were common whereas cancer was very rare.[82]

A second cause of population decline is family limitation. These were uncertain times and family limitation may have been practiced by the simple expedient of not entering into or at least delaying partnerships or marriage until later in life. This reduction in the fertile period of the woman could have a significant effect on the number of children produced.

Domesday Book appears to be a source on which calculations of population can be based. Godmanchester's 80 villeins and 16 bordars imply a population of just under 500. This is little different from the higher of the two estimates of population for the Roman period. However, Domesday Book was not intended to be a population census.[83] Domesday is notorious for omitting information. Sub tenants who did not pay rent, the landless and certain other groups like craftsmen were not recorded. For example, Godmanchester's three mills would have had millers but no millers are included in Godmanchester's entry. Allowing for omissions in Domesday, Godmanchester's population in the late eleventh century was probably somewhere between 500 and an upper limit of about 800.

The following two centuries witnessed a rapid growth of the population. The population of towns grew even more rapidly rising from about 10 per cent of England's population at Domesday to at least 15 per cent by the fourteenth century.[84] Immediately prior to the Black Death, England's population had reached a peak of between four and six millions. This was at least three times greater than it had been two-and-a-half centuries earlier and it was putting great stress on the country's ability to feed its people.[85] This growth in population is reflected in the Hundred Roll of Godmanchester for 1279.[86] An inquiry at the instigation of King Edward I, the hundred rolls provide details of each manor, the types of land and their associated rights and numbers of both free and unfree tenants. The records for Huntingdonshire including those for Godmanchester are very well preserved.[87] Although these records are complex, they record over 450 landholders for Godmanchester suggesting a population of around 2,000.[88] In the fourteenth century, tax returns suggest that Huntingdonshire had a population of over 48,000 and with an estimated population of 131 per square mile was the third most densely populated county in the country.[89] Godmanchester's population peak during the high Middle Ages would not be reached again until the nineteenth century.

One of the most momentous events to hit Godmanchester was the Black Death. Tales of the rapid spread of 'the pestilence' across Europe would have reached Godmanchester but any hope that the English Channel would halt its advance was false. On the contrary, it was sea routes which facilitated its advance. In the summer of 1348, bubonic plague arrived in the south and west of England and it would kill about half the population. The plague spread rapidly arriving in London by the autumn and then on into East Anglia. It would have reached Godmanchester by the early summer in 1349. The catastrophe of the Black Death resulted in a fall of about half of the population and it took five centuries for Godmanchester's population to return to pre-Black Death levels.

The Black Death created panic. Few doubted that the pestilence was sent by God and most interpreted it as a punishment for sin. But why was God so angry with the world in the fourteenth century? People were desperate to discover how God's anger could be assuaged. But prayers, confessions and absolutions not only had no impact on its rapid advance but the disease mutated into a still worse pneumonic form. If God was punishing sin, then it seems that his particular targets were labourers and children. No social group was spared but the elite experienced significantly lower death rates than labourers. As a result few were left to work the land and despite attempts to control wages, shortage of labour was so great that wages inevitably rose. The pestilence did not stay away for long and returned in 1361 and again in 1369. In these years it was children who experienced the highest death rates.

From the early modern period onwards population levels can be estimated from parish registers, diocesan records, tax returns and census records. In 1538, Thomas Cromwell ordered every parish in England and Wales to maintain a register of baptisms, marriages and burials. Initially, normal practice was to record these events on loose sheets many of which have been destroyed.[90] A brief entry in Godmanchester's Churchwardens accounts in the sixteenth century records a payment of 4 pence for a quire of paper for the 'Regester boke'.[91] Only 10 per cent of registers survive from 1538.[92] Godmanchester's parish registers commence in 1604 and diocesan population returns for the years 1563, 1603, 1705 and 1723 survive. The hearth tax was a property tax on dwellings, graded according to the number of their fireplaces.[93] Hearth tax returns for 1664 and 1674 purport to record all households for Godmanchester including those exempt from paying the tax. Therefore if a reasonable estimate of average household size can be established populations can be calculated from these tax records.

Unfortunately, there are many problems with interpreting parish registers and tax records. Parish priests were not primarily employed to keep registers and some suffer from clergy neglect or incapacity. Registers did not always promptly record events and this led to forgetting names or omitting events altogether.[94] Rites of passage were not confined to the Church of England and baptisms were not the same as births as a result of delays in baptising babies. Infant mortality rates were high and infants not publicly baptised were unregistered. Hearth tax returns did not always record exempt households consistently and therefore unwary users of these records could easily underestimate population levels.

There was a steep increase in England's population in the second half of the sixteenth century but in the second half of the seventeenth century the population was static. Based on hearth tax returns, Godmanchester's population was somewhere between 1250 and 1500 in 1674, still substantially less than three centuries earlier. In 1674 Godmanchester had the third highest population of any parish in Huntingdonshire, below Ramsey and St Ives but higher than Huntingdon. Density of population can also be inferred from hearth tax returns. This suggests a significant pattern of relatively dense settlement in the Ouse Valley including Godmanchester.

By the nineteenth century, the relative size of parishes in Huntingdonshire changed. Based on census returns for 1841, Huntingdon had become the largest town in the county with a population of 3507. St Ives followed closely behind with 3465 people but Godmanchester with 2152 people had only 61 per cent of Huntingdon's population in 1841 when in 1674 it had stood at 130 per cent of Huntingdon's population.[95] During the nineteenth and twentieth centuries when national population grew rapidly, Godman-

WHO WERE THE PEOPLE? | 49

chester experienced very little growth. In 1971 the population still only stood at 3115.

Since 1971 the town has experienced the fastest growth in its history and the population has doubled to over 6,000. Further large increases in population are projected for the town. Average household size has continued to reduce and is now only 2.3 people, the same as for the nation as a whole but only half of what it was in the seventeenth century. The people of Godmanchester were captured for posterity when the Millennium was celebrated in the Year 2000. Photographs of its inhabitants were taken by a team of volunteers and these are to be deposited in the County Record Office.

Social Structure

When historians write about social structure it usually reveals a great deal about their presuppositions or some would say prejudices. For example Marxist historians usually see society as consisting of two conflicting interests. So in the medieval period Marxist historians perceive a battle between elite landowners exploiting peasant farmers by driving up their rents and reducing labourers' wages. However, in reality society does not consist of two opposing groups but a wide spectrum of people with many gradations of power, status and wealth. Even gentry can be down on their luck with hardly any assets remaining whereas some labourers could be relatively prosperous. Society is not inherently in conflict and there was much social co-operation.

One view of medieval society saw a clear distinction between three orders. At the top were those who pray (*oratores*) followed by those who wage war (*bellatores*) and underneath them the vast majority who worked (*laboratores*). Those who worked were mostly employed in agriculture and the various ranks of society were identified by their relationship to the land. Godmanchester like the country as a whole was a hierarchical society. Chapter four set out the relationship between the 'unfree' population and their lord and the changes brought about by the Charter of 1212. Godmanchester's 'unfree' population had many more relatively prosperous villeins than bordars. In 1212 the population became free tenants. The social hierarchy in Godmanchester continued to be mainly based on agriculture and towards the end of the medieval period there was a hierarchy of gentry, yeomen, husbandmen and labourers. A simplistic explanation would suggest that the gentry were landowners who did not work themselves, yeomen farmed larger farms, husbandmen were tenants of smaller farms and labourers worked for others. Life is rarely so straightforward.

Gentry were not a legally defined group in society and by the early modern period comprised a wide range of people with a wide range of incomes.[96] John Bedells used heralds' visitation returns to assess the number of gentry in Huntingdonshire. The two visitations for Huntingdonshire in the seventeenth century were held in 1613 and 1684. Although there were certain 'indisputable qualifications' for gentry status such as the sovereign's commission, a call to the Bar or a university degree, there was a considerable degree of dispute as to who should be accepted as a gentleman. The 1613 visitation accepted 60 families living in forty eight different parishes in Huntingdonshire and 53 gentry families in 1684. These numbers would suggest that gentry households represented just over one per cent of Huntingdonshire households.[97] For William Harrison an essential element of gentry status was that gentlemen were those who 'can live without manual labour'.[98] Sir Thomas Overbury described the important difference between yeomen and gentlemen by writing that the yeoman 'even though he be master, says not to his servants go to the field but let us go'.[99]

During the latter Middle Ages the term yeomen came to mean an intermediary social category between husbandman and gentry. But by the early modern period, yeomen were not always easy to define because of variations in their wealth and size of their farms. This is demonstrated by probate inventory values of yeomen in Huntingdonshire. These amounts represent the values of deceased persons' goods, their farm animals and crops and debts due to them at their death. However property and debts owing are not included and therefore they are only approximate guides to relative wealth. At the top end of the spectrum were yeomen who had inventoried wealth in excess of almost all the inventoried gentry. At the opposite end were yeomen with little inventoried wealth who were frequently much poorer than husbandmen and even the occasional labourer.

TABLE 1: YEOMEN INVENTORY VALUES		
Huntingdonshire (1609-1723)		
	No.	%
>£1000	2	2
£500-£1000	2	2
£250-£500	15	13
£100-£250	39	36
<£100	51	47
Totals	109	100

The word 'husbandmen' was literally a person engaged in husbandry, tending animals and tilling the soil.[100] In 1613, the English writer Gervase Markham wrote, 'A husbandman is he which with discretion and good order tilleth the ground in his due seasons, making it fruitfull to bring forth corne, and plants, meete for the sustenance of man'.[101] A husbandman was a small-to-middling farmer for whom life was a struggle, always vulnerable to economic disaster but who could expect to get by in all but the very worst years.[102] Husbandmen typically farmed between five and fifty acres.[103] Such plots were defined by historian Keith Wrightson as holdings supporting a family and producing a modest surplus in most years. These small holdings relied for the most part on family labour.[104]

In 1688 the civil servant Gregory King estimated that 'labourers, cottagers and paupers' and their families comprised 46 per cent of the population.[105] For Keith Wrightson, the most striking feature of King's calculation was the 'yawning gap' between the yearly income of the least well off of the 'middle sort' and those of labouring people.[106] King estimated the annual income of a farmer's family to be £42 10s whereas families of labourers and servants had £15 and cottagers and paupers only £6 10s.[107] However, the nearly half of the population included by King in his category 'labourers, cottagers and paupers' embraced a wide range of people from labourers who owned some land, animals and crops to paupers. Keith Wrightson suggested that more fortunate labourers might hold an acre or two or enjoy the benefits of customary common rights.[108]

Most labourers did not work land on their own account but worked for other people. Economic historian Gregory Clark published day wages of labourers for each individual year and by decade from 1200 to 1869. (Table 2)

TABLE 2: DAY WAGES OF AGRICULTURAL LABOURERS		
Decade	Estimated Day wage	Purchasing power
	(d./day)	1860-9=100
1200-9	1.4	69
1300-9	1.3	45
1340-9	1.5	51
1350-9	2.7	75
1400-9	3.4	107
1450-9	3.8	126
1600-9	7.6	66
1650-9	10.1	66
1700-9	10.2	72
1750-9	10.9	70
1790-9	15.6	72
1860-9	23.4	100

Clark's data shows the effect of the Black Death on labourers' wages and standard of living. The purchasing power of labourers' pay was relatively low in the early fourteenth century as labour supply was plentiful. In the decade following the Black Death their wage rates sharply increased by 80 per cent. Furthermore as a result of depressed demand, falling prices of food particularly grain and meat in the fifteenth century meant that labourers' living standards doubled. However, calculating wages in the distant past is not a straightforward enterprise. Wage rates varied regionally and seasonally, not all labourers had the same skills and part of their wages was in kind. Keith Wrightson estimated that a labourer's wage represented about 12d for a day's work in the seventeenth century whereas according to Clark, day rates did not reach this level until 1767.[109] Examination of nominal wages without reference to purchasing power can be misleading. For example, the nominal value of an agricultural labourer's wage increased from 7.6*d* in 1600-1609 to 15.6*d* in 1790-1799 but the purchasing power of those wages hardly increased at all during the seventeenth and eighteenth centuries.[110]

Occupation had been the basis of social classification since at least 1413. In that year an Act of Parliament required original writs to identify an individual's estate or degree. One problem in complying with this legislation was that many people had more than one occupation. The large number of surnames that reflect an occupation such as carpenter, tailor, baker and tanner is a reminder that men were defined by their occupation.

Women were defined by their marital status although this should not disguise the fact that they carried out a multitude of jobs. The shortage of labour created by the Black Death meant that women were no longer confined to less well paid work such as spinning and wool combing. They expanded into weaving and demanded higher pay for more traditional female employment such as weeding and harvesting. Women engaged in trade and sold food and drink, particularly ale. When their husbands died they often took over their trades. Despite these advances their social status always remained inferior to men.[111]

As the economy developed in the early modern period the percentage of the workforce employed on the land decreased. There was a significant increase in the numbers of people employed in various trades and crafts. This was particularly the case in urban areas and even in small towns like Godmanchester. The principal trades were concerned with food and drink (innkeepers, victuallers, bakers and butchers) clothing (tailors, cordwainers and glovers) and building (bricklayers and carpenters). Probate records show that many such tradesmen lived in Godmanchester. Some tradesmen were very wealthy particularly tanners and millers.

Where did these tradesmen fit in the social hierarchy? The historian Lorna Weatherill suggested that occupations of 'high status' such as clergy, apothecaries and doctors and also occupations of 'intermediate status' such as innkeepers, malsters and tanners had a social status between gentry and yeomen. For Weatherill trades of 'low status' such as butchers, bakers and cordwainers fell between yeomen and husbandmen.[112] One problem with this approach was that almost all occupational descriptors could embrace a wide range of people. For example, a cordwainer could be a relatively poor person who worked for somebody else or the owner of a substantial business. Contemporary writers in early modern England often used terms such 'the better sort' or the 'poorer sort' of people. The better sort' were middling ranks and the poorer sort largely labourers, cottagers and paupers.

Another approach towards constructing a social hierarchy is to use probate inventory values. (Table 3)

TABLE 3: SOCIAL HIERARCHY BASED ON INVENTORY VALUES
1. Tanners
2. Apothecaries / Doctors
3. Shopkeepers
4. Clergy
5. Glovers
6. Innkeepers
7. Bakers
8. Clothiers / Clothworkers
9. Blacksmiths
10. Cordwainers / Shoemakers
11. Carpenters / Joiners
12. Masons
13. Weavers
14. Butchers
15. Tailors
16. Bricklayers

Probate inventory values were a statement of gross wealth of individuals but exclude land and property and also debts owed by deceased persons. In the late seventeenth and eighteenth centuries, some tradesmen such as tanners appear to be relatively prosperous whereas tailors and bricklayers owned much fewer goods.

In a rapidly changing society, establishing a person's place in the social hierarchy was very contentious. Some historians such as Mark Overton have argued that the most important determinant of status was possession, and particularly ownership of land.[113] Others have suggested that several criteria determined social rank including birth, wealth, occupation and lifestyle.[114] These criteria were often in conflict and one area where this conflict was frequently revealed was in church. The layout of pews in church reflected the hierarchical structure of society.[115] Prestigious pews were located close to the pulpit and so eminent men sat at the front and poorer men towards the back. There were often battles between neighbours and presentments by churchwardens about seat allocation arrangements.[116] Some churches even went so far as providing two grades of communion wine; muscatel or malmsey for the 'better sort' and claret for the others.[117] However, one further reason why a person's place in the social hierarchy was contentious was because an individual's circumstance could change. If relative status related to wealth, this opened the door to both upward and downward social mobility. There was little financial security in the early modern period for people were vulnerable to sickness, fire, bad harvests and other threats.

A further source which gives an insight into social structure in the seventeenth century is hearth tax returns. With the restoration of the monarchy in 1660 efforts were made to provide the king with sufficient income to avoid future conflicts with Parliament. This led to the introduction of the Hearth Tax in 1662 a property tax on dwellings, graded according to the number of their fireplaces.[118] Hearth tax returns for both 1664 and 1674 survive for Huntingdonshire. The tax was levied at the rate of two shillings per hearth per annum. The tax had to be paid at Lady Day (25 March, the official start of the year until 1752) and Michaelmas (29 September, the feast of St Michael the Archangel). Although not without problems, the number of hearths per household was a rough guide to the social structure of a community. Table 4 shows the number and percentage of hearths in four categories in respect of five market towns in Huntingdonshire. Huntingdon, the county town, clearly had a different social structure to the other four towns. In 1674, no less than 19 per cent of Huntingdon's properties had six or more hearths. Godmanchester had only 5 per cent of its properties with six or more hearths. Nevertheless 30 per cent of Godmanchester's households had 3 or more hearths which was higher than the average in England.

TABLE 4: SOCIAL COMPOSITION OF FIVE HUNTINGDONSHIRE PARISHES											
1664	Huntingdon		St Ives		Kimbolton		Ramsey		Godmanchester		Totals	
Hearths	No.	%	No.	%	No.	%	No.	%	No.	%	No.	%
6+	24	17	17	8	6	6	5	3	3	3	55	8
3-5	46	33	65	29	24	23	28	18	38	36	201	27
2	37	27	42	19	28	27	77	49	53	50	237	33
1	32	23	96	44	45	44	46	30	11	11	230	32
Total	139	100	220	100	103	100	156	100	105	100	723	100
3+	70	50	82	37	30	29	33	21	41	39	256	35
1674	Huntingdon		St Ives		Kimbolton		Ramsey		Godmanchester		Totals	
Hearths	No.	%	No.	%	No.	%	No.	%	No.	%	No.	%
6+	36	19	16	7	6	5	7	3	12	5	77	8
3-5	48	25	75	33	32	27	39	15	55	25	249	25
2	50	26	43	19	33	28	67	27	52	23	245	24
1	56	30	92	41	48	40	138	55	103	46	437	43
Total	190	100	226	100	119	100	251	100	222	100	1008	100
3+	84	44	91	40	38	32	46	18	67	30	326	33

In the nineteenth century insights into social structure can be gleaned from census returns. In 1851, by far the most common occupation in Huntingdonshire was an agricultural labourer. There were 8886 agricultural labourers and farm servants compared to a total of 5179 people employed in the next 12 most commonly recorded occupations. Agricultural labourers represented poorly paid manual labour. In Godmanchester, forty years on the pattern is broadly similar with the majority of the employed population being labourers. However, in Godmanchester there were more labourers employed in areas other than agriculture such as milling, brewing and brickmaking than in the County as a whole. (Table 5)

TABLE 5: OCCUPATIONS IN THE NINETEENTH CENTURY		
	Huntingdonshire 1851 Census	Godmanchester 1891 Census
Male Occupations	No.	No.
Agricultural Labourers/ Servants	8886	94
Farmers	966	25
Labourers	837	79
Shoemakers	639	8
Carpenter/Joiners	450	12
Tailors	393	3
Bricklayers	360	5
Gardeners	302	10
Blacksmiths	278	3
Butchers	262	3
Bakers	242	9
Brickmakers	235	11
Railway Labourers	215	20

In the recent past, politicians have frequently expressed aspirations of achieving a more equal society. Nevertheless social hierarchies remain. The Registrar General continues to use seven socio-economic groups ranging from class one, professionals to classes five and six, unskilled and others. Categorising people into social groups contains as many problems today as it did in the early modern period.

6

THE ECONOMY

Agriculture

In the Middle Ages at least three quarters of England's national income came from agriculture and agricultural products. Agriculture employed the majority of the labour force, much of the capital and a great deal of the management talent.[119] As the previous chapter has shown, agriculture was the mainstay of Godmanchester's economy for most of its history. Godmanchester was one of the largest agricultural settlements in Huntingdonshire throughout the medieval period.[120]

The traditional farming year began after harvest when the arable land was ploughed and harrowed. The land was ploughed in ridges and furrows to help drainage. Oxen were originally used for ploughing but were gradually replaced by horses. Using horses was far more efficient because they could work one and a half times faster than oxen and thus reduce labour inputs. Ploughing turned over the soil burying the stubble and weeds and leaving the bare soil exposed. If the land had been used for a previous arable crop it would typically be ploughed four times but six times if the land had been under pasture. After ploughing the land would be harrowed to make a tilth so that the seed could be sown. If it was to be used for a spring crop the land would not be harrowed until the spring. Winter cereals (wheat and rye) were sown in September and October and spring crops (barley, oats and peas) were sown between February and April. The sower walked across the field with a basket full of seed and scattered the seed by hand. The seed would then be covered by harrowing again. Weeds were kept down by intensive labour. Winter grains were harvested before the spring crops. Wheat and rye were reaped with a small hook called a sickle and barley and oats mown with a larger scythe. The crop was then bound into sheaves. Threshing took place to extract the grain. Winnowing separated grain from the chaff and sieving separated weeds from the cereal grain. Finally grain was put in sacks and taken to the miller. The best bread was made from wheat. Barley was used for malt to make ale, some bread and also animal feed. Oats were for both human and animal consumption. The sowing and sheep inventory taken in 1334 revealed that slightly more than a third of the total sown acreage in Godmanchester was barley and more than a third was peas. The remainder was divided between wheat, oats, rye and dredge.[121]

Arable land was divided into strips in open fields with no hedges or fences. The open field system was probably introduced in the eighth and ninth centuries. It aimed to control the balance between arable and live-stock farming and to ensure a reasonable distribution of the quality of land amongst the community. By dividing the land into strips the good and bad land was shared out. Crops were rotated and animals grazed on the stubble after the harvest and on the fallow, with communal controls on their numbers to prevent over grazing.

Godmanchester had six open fields.[122] The West and East Commons either side of East Field were used by the freemen for grazing stock.

BOX 1 GODMANCHESTER'S OPEN FIELDS	
Open Fields	**Location**
West Field	West of Offord Road
Forest Field	Between London Road and Offord Road
Depden Field	Beyond Forest Field to the west of the A1198 and leading up to Lattenbury Hill
East Field	East of Cambridge Road
Basscroft	East of London Road
East Garden Field	Between Cambridge Road and London Road

The pastoral farming year began in spring with lambing and calving. Hay was harvested in June and July when grass was mown with a scythe and left to dry. In September and October bulls serviced cows and rams serviced ewes. Daily activities included milking cows and processing milk into cheese and butter.

At the time of King John's Charter prices for agricultural produce were rising and landowners farmed the land themselves rather than letting out their land to tenants at fixed rents. By the beginning of the fourteenth century the very high level of population in England had left people struggling to survive. Relatively poor land was brought into cultivation and the living standards of the majority were at an extremely low level. This was further exacerbated by the climate which became much colder and wetter. The evidence for this significant climate change can be clearly seen in the Greenland ice core samples and the growth records of British oak trees. The harvest failed repeatedly in the years 1315-21. Both winter and spring crop yields plummeted and the price of grain rocketed. To cap it all cattle plague spread from central Europe and arrived in England in 1319. The purchasing power of wages reached their lowest levels in 700 years and many experienced famine. Petty landowners sold their plots of land to buy food and many turned to crime.[123] All this was to change as a result of the Black Death, one of the greatest turning points in English history. It is said that every cloud has a silver lining. This was true for those who managed to survive.

The calamitous drop in population meant that young people were able to establish a landholding much more easily and at an earlier stage of their lives. Land holdings generally increased in size. There was also a shortage of labour and as a result the real value of wages rose sharply. This led to a significant rise in living standards and now labourers could afford the best bread and more meat than before. According to the contemporary poet William Langland even beggars refused inferior quality bread and demanded white bread and the best ale! Attempts to control the labour market and to restrict wages under the Statute of Labourers of 1351 were unsuccessful. People would not agree to work at pre-plague rates for their bargaining position had radically changed. In a matter of weeks shortage of land had changed into an oversupply and now labour was so scarce that previously unheard of rates of pay were being agreed. Labourers could leave their local manor and there was little that the lord of the manor could do about it. A recorded case at nearby Hemingford Abbots revealed the attempt by the lord of the manor, the Abbot of Ramsey to recall Simon Duntyng from Daventry. He ordered his relatives to bring him back with threats of financial penalties. But all to no avail.[124]

When the first poll tax was introduced in 1377 the government thought it was only reasonable that at least some of the 'exorbitant' wage demands of labourers should be clawed back. The poll tax of 1380 was set at a shilling, about three days' pay. The poll tax, which was intended to help pay for the war effort against France, brought wage earners previously exempted from payment into the tax system. The shock that tax demands should be applied to everyone over fifteen years old led to the Peasants Revolt of 1381. Parallels have frequently been drawn to the response to the introduction of the Poll Tax six centuries later in 1990.

In many communities the response to the shortage of labour was to reduce arable farming and switch to animal husbandry which required significantly less manpower. Wool became one of the most important commodities in the English economy and clothmaking developed in many parts of the country. A peasant economy started to be transformed into a capitalist economy paving the way for the agricultural and industrial revolutions.

At some point after the mid-sixteenth century an agricultural revolution took place which enabled the rapidly rising population of England to be fed. Historians endlessly debate the date of this revolution. Estimates suggest that agricultural output more than trebled between 1700 and 1850 and by the mid-nineteenth century output per worker was over double that of any other European state.[125] The factors that brought about this revolution are also controversial. However, there is little doubt that changing technology had a role to play and agriculture became far more efficient thus releasing manpower for more diversified economic activity. The introduction of turnips and clover enabled new crop rotations which reduced the need for fallow. Livestock was improved and convertible husbandry practiced so that advantage could be taken of changes in the relative prices of meat and cereals. Not all of these improvements took place in Godmanchester. At the end of the eighteenth century a traditional three year rotation of wheat, legumes and fallow was still in operation.

There is a way to determine the balance of arable and pastoral farming in a parish. Predominately arable parishes had a high proportion of autumn marriages following the harvest and predominately pastoral parishes had a high proportion of spring and early summer marriages following lambing and calving. Marriages in parishes with high levels of rural industry had no distinct seasonal marriage patterns.[126] Based on this hypothesis we analysed marriage registers of five Huntingdonshire parishes by month of marriage. Our analysis showed that marriages in four parishes including Godmanchester peaked in the autumn but Ramsey marriages peaked in both spring and autumn.[127]

TABLE 6: MARRIAGE INDICES BY PARISH		
Period 1701-1725		
Parish	AUTUMN	SPRING
Kimbolton	193	125
Godmanchester	156	114
Huntingdon	163	111
St Ives	156	102
Ramsey	166	144

Analysis of surviving seventeenth and eighteenth-century inventories for these five parishes confirmed that whereas Kimbolton and Godmanchester were principally arable Ramsey had mixed arable and pastoral farming.

In the early fourteenth century, ownership of land was concentrated in very few hands. The wealth of the church was staggering. Half the land of England was owned by the church, principally the 826 religious houses including Ramsey Abbey, one of the wealthiest monasteries in England. The other half was owned by the Earls, Barons, Knights, Gentry and of course the king. Archbishops and bishops typically received the same level of income from the land as an earl.[128] More than a century after the Black Death, land holding in Godmanchester can be traced. The vital source document is the farm rentals for Michaelmas 1485 which has been extensively analysed by J. Ambrose Raftis.

BOX 2: POLARISED LANDHOLDINGS IN GODMANCHESTER IN 1485	
Size of landholding acres	Landholders number
50+	28
21-50	44
11-20	34
10 or less	144
Total	250

More than half (57%) of landholders in Godmanchester held 10 acres or less. The largest landholding was the church, the Prior of Merton with 168 acres. In Godmanchester, land passed to the youngest and not the oldest surviving male child. This system of inheritance known as Borough English was practiced in a number of counties including Kent, Norfolk, Suffolk, Surrey and Sussex.

A further major change in landholding occurred when the Parish of Godmanchester was enclosed in 1803.[129] The open fields were enclosed by hedges and fences and land was concentrated in far fewer hands. The enclosure map for Godmanchester survives. Whether enclosure was a good or a bad thing is a matter of controversy. John Clare, the Northamptonshire poet worked as a hedge setter, a day labourer and was gardener at Burghley House from 1810 to 1811. He had no doubt that enclosure was bad. Clare wrote:

> Enclosure came, and trampled on the grave
> Of labour's rights and left the poor man a slave.

In the early twentieth century, left-wing historians Barbara and John Hammond argued that enclosure destroyed the fabric of village life. It was fatal to the small farmer, cottagers and squatters. The loss of opportunities for the landless to gather fuel and graze animals on common land was significant. For example keeping a cow on the commons could be worth up to six months cash wages for an agricultural labourer. Furthermore a woman could often glean three or four bushels of wheat which represented about two week's wages.[130] The Marxist historian E. P. Thompson writing in the 1960s concluded that enclosure was 'a plain enough case of class robbery'.

However, there were many benefits of enclosure. Some historians have argued that Parliamentary enclosure was fundamental to the 'agricultural revolution' for enclosure made it easier to control the land and therefore led to more efficient agriculture. The population was rising to unprecedented levels and much more food needed to be produced or starvation would result. In the event, agricultural yields rose and the people were fed but the extent to which enclosure contributed to increasing agricultural production is a matter of vigorous historical debate. In Godmanchester, the new field systems can be seen on the enclosure map held in the new Archives centre in Huntingdon. One of the biggest landowners was Henry Sweeting and Sweetings Road which leads into a large housing development begun in the 1980s was named after him.

Farming in the Nineteenth Century

At the end of the Napoleonic War with France in 1815, cheap corn flooded into the country. Many English farmers were faced with bankruptcy. Lord Liverpool's government responded by introducing the Corn Laws. The legislation banned the import of wheat unless the price of home-grown wheat reached the very high price of 80 shillings a quarter-hundredweight. Protecting farmers also meant high bread prices which led to riots in several parts of the country.

Following poor harvests in three consecutive years 1828-30 there were 'Swing riots' in many agricultural counties including Huntingdonshire. The name derived from letters signed by 'Captain Swing' which were sent to farmers and manufacturers threatening destruction of their property if they did not either remove the new threshing machines or increase their wages. Eric Evans also interprets the riots as a protest against the elite in society for failing in their traditional paternalistic duties in looking after the basic needs of agricultural workers.[131] In any event the penalties imposed on labourers were harsh although capital punishment was commuted to transportation in most cases. The Huntingdonshire Quarter Sessions records contain a number of references to Huntingdonshire men found guilty of destroying threshing machines in 1830 and consequently sentenced to transportation to Australia.[132]

The 1870s were a period of agricultural hardship, particularly in the east of England. Cheap wheat from North America and imports of cheap wool from Australia provided stiff competition for British farmers. Furthermore inclement weather led to poor harvests and 1879 was one of the wettest years on record. When the Prime Minister Disraeli took a walk in a storm he came across a group of farmers and asked them 'if the dove had left the ark yet'. The continued wet weather of the following two years led to sheep rot, causing a loss of no less than six million animals in the country. Arable farming was hit particularly hard as the price of wheat fell by more than half between 1870 and the beginning of the twentieth century. As a result of poor returns available to arable farmers, the acreage devoted to wheat production in Britain fell sharply. In 1851, 78 per cent of wheat was home produced but this had fallen to below 25 per cent by the turn of the twentieth century. The United States, India, Russia and Argentina filled the gap.[133] Each Easter week a fair was held in Godmanchester but by the beginning of the twentieth century it was a shadow of its former self. In 1905 *The Hunts Post* reported sadly that a good price was obtained for a few superior horses but there was not much call for the inferior sort. Trade was slow and there was an entire absence of Welsh ponies which had formerly been a feature of the market.

British farmers continued to experience a period of depression until 1940 as a result of increasing world food supplies and competition from cheaper producers.[134] Perry argued that Huntingdonshire was the heartland of this agricultural depression with a high level of farms failing.[135] Agricultural workers wages remained much lower than average wages. However income is not the sole measure of living standards. Life expectancy was much higher in rural areas than in cities. For example in 1861-70, life expectancy at birth was 46.5 years in rural England but only 33 years in large cities outside London.[136] Those who left Godmanchester for the bright lights of urban living might have enjoyed higher wages but high death rates and crowded living hardly improved their lot in life.

The onset of the Second World War meant that demand for home produced food increased dramatically. I. B. Hunter who lived in Almond Close worked for Teddy Page at Tudor Farm during the school holidays. He recalls that Mr Page employed at least 15 men and several boys during harvest time and that it was always hard work. Wheat and barley was stacked in the fields and the boys also returned loads to the farm to be stacked there. There were barns at the rear of Tudor Farm and several stables in which Italian and German prisoners of war slept.[137]

Trades and Crafts

Even before the Black Death, Godmanchester had a number of tradesmen living in the town. They included carpenters, butchers, bakers, millers, tanners, weavers, candle makers, masons and fishermen.[138] In the late 15th century increasing numbers of tradesmen and craftsmen were recorded in tax records known as lay subsidy rolls. For example, a shoemaker, John Hawkyn, is recorded as living in Arnyng Street. This did not mean that many of these people followed these occupations on a full time basis. The focus of Godmanchester's economy remained largely agricultural and people employed in various trades and crafts also engaged in agriculture. By-employment, or having more than one occupation, was common and was not just a survival strategy for the poor. For example, probate records of tradesmen and craftsmen record not just the tools of their trade but also relatively high levels of ownership of animals and crops. One reason why the term 'farmer' was not commonly used until the eighteenth century was that most male adults practised farming.[139]

Godmanchester was different to many other Huntingdonshire parishes for it was a small town and had a market. There are occasional references to Godmanchester's market such as in the bailiffs' accounts for 1533. In 1615, fish was brought to Godmanchester market on Fridays.[140] The actual location of the market is not recorded but it is likely to be close to the river.

There is not space to consider all of the trades practised in Godmanchester. The surviving probate inventories for the town relating to the seventeenth and eighteenth centuries record 32 different non-agricultural occupations. One trade, tanning, is of particular interest because it shows how tradesmen could have very considerable amounts of money invested in their trade and as a result appear to have considerable wealth often exceeding that of the gentry. The extent to which these assets were financed by borrowing must also be taken into consideration for any true estimate of their wealth to be made.

Tanners needed substantial premises and made considerable investments in hides before achieving a return. Tanners bought hides from butchers after animals were slaughtered and sold their skins after tanning to shoemakers and glovers. Skins were prepared for de-fleshing and removal of hair by a first immersion in a suspension of lime. After scraping they were re-limed in order to open up the grain structure. Finally they were de-limed by soaking in dung or vegetable liquors. After washing they underwent a lengthy tanning stage in pits containing water and oak bark.[141] Heavy cattle skins required a longer period for processing than lighter skins from sheep, goats and calves. The whole process could take up to eighteen months for high quality leather.

Several members of the Negus family in Godmanchester were tanners in the eighteenth century. Of all the surviving probate inventories for Godmanchester that were considered by the Archdeaconry Court in the seventeenth and eighteenth centuries, the highest recorded valuation was for William Negus. The valuation was no less than £1351 in 1709. To put this figure in context, an agricultural labourer, would have typically earned just under a shilling a day in 1709. Annual rates are difficult to calculate because numbers of days worked by labourers varied. Demand for labour was seasonal and irregular with peak periods at lambing, harvesting and haymaking and slack periods from November to February. Furthermore, labourers often received payments in kind as well as in cash. However, a labourer would be unlikely to earn more than about £15 in 1709. William Negus is recorded as a gentleman in his probate inventory but he was clearly engaged in tanning for his inventory lists hides and other stocks valued at £550. John Negus who died in 1749 had hides, skins and bark in his 'tanyard' valued at £336.

The Industrial Revolution

The agricultural revolution in England paved the way for an industrial revolution. However, the changes in industrial production largely passed Huntingdonshire by as the county like many other areas remained mainly agricultural. Nevertheless Huntingdonshire was not immune to the results of economic changes taking place in other parts of the country. Eighteenth-century Huntingdonshire witnessed the beginning of a consumer revolution in which the middle ranks of society began to own a range of goods including clocks, knives and forks, mirrors, china and tea and coffee pots.

The results of this consumer revolution can be seen in the probate records of Godmanchester residents. Examination of these records for the latter half of the eighteenth century reveals a quite different world from those of the seventeenth century. In 1782 John Seward died. He was a hostler, someone employed in a stable to take care of the horses. John left very modest possessions: three beds and their bedding, a few tables and chairs some pewter and brass but also a clock valued at no less than £2. The clock valuation represented more than 10 per cent of the value of all his recorded possessions. The following year Richard Crofts a basketmaker died. The total value of his possessions at £23 were little more than those of John Seward. Like many craftsmen he also engaged in agriculture for his most valuable possessions were his two cows. But like John Seward he was also the owner of a clock which was displayed in his kitchen. When Edmund Simons died in 1784 his occupation was not recorded. He was clearly of superior social status to Crofts and Seward for his possessions totalled £282, two thirds of which was money in his purse. Edmund's inventory recorded most of the new consumer goods: a clock, a watch, 12 knives and forks, a coffee mill, two tea pots, a tea kettle, tea boards, a tea chest, and window curtains.

A sample of three probate inventories is insufficient to establish evidence of a consumer revolution. Godmanchester on its own does not have sufficient surviving records to provide a sufficient sample. However, by examining the county as a whole a robust sample of probate inventories can be assembled. Table 7 is based on examination of no less than 1423 probate inventories.

TABLE 7: CLOCK OWNERSHIP IN HUNTINGDONSHIRE				
	1600-1649	1650-1699	1700-1749	1750-1800
	%	%	%	%
Gentry	0	14	60	67
Yeomen	0	8	27	58
Husbandmen	0	0	45	33
Labourers	0	0	1	57
Widows	0	1	10	47
Professionals	0	9	29	33
Higher status tradesmen	0	3	32	63
Lower status tradesmen	0	1	18	59

It shows how a 'consumer revolution' extended to lower ranks, many of whom also began to own a range of new goods such as domestic clocks. Although the gentry owned more elaborate and expensive clocks probate records show that ownership of clocks spread rapidly to include even the more affluent labourers in the county. The records undermine the Marxist historian, E.P. Thompson's assertion that no labourer could have afforded a clock in the mid-eighteenth century.

Shops

The way goods were distributed also changed. In pre-industrial rural society goods were mainly purchased from markets or itinerant traders. By 1700, retail shops were becoming more common but traditional retailing still continued at periodical markets and by hawkers and peddlers.[142] The new shops catered mainly for wealthier classes and so a person's rank was decisive in the type of retailer patronised. Smaller shops which sold groceries, household goods and clothing increased in number during the eighteenth century. Shops selling clothing were the most common. They comprised drapers, haberdashers, hatters, hosiers and milliners, breeches and stay makers and tailors. Based on excise records, historians Mui and Mui calculated that there were 141,700 shops in England and Wales in 1759, an average of 46 people per shop. This ratio of population to shops varied in different parts of the country with only 28 people per shop in the Home Counties but 110 people per shop in Wales. Huntingdonshire and Cambridgeshire with 36 people per shop had a relatively high number of shops.[143]

Another source of evidence for the spread of shops is trade tokens. Trade tokens were used as small change. More than 2,000 shopkeepers issued trade tokens between 1649 and 1672 and these shopkeepers were located in 822 places. The places were very unevenly distributed with Kent, Suffolk and Yorkshire having the highest numbers. Many small places had token-issuing shopkeepers including Godmanchester. These have been studied in depth by Gary Oddie. The Norris Museum, St Ives holds examples from Godmanchester including those issued by Robert Carles (RC) a grocer, and Samuel Connye (SC) who was possibly an innkeeper.

Godmanchester trade tokens from the seventeenth century (Courtesy Gary Oddie)

When Island Cottage in Post Street was recently refurbished, writing on the jetty was revealed. It advertised the goods for sale including snuff, tea, coffee and pepper, revealing that the building had previously been used as a shop. Further research may provide evidence of the period when the shop was in business. By the early twentieth century Godmanchester had a wide range of shops and tradesmen and these are listed in Kelly's Directory for 1910. They included Frederick Bird draper, William Childs fishmonger, Markham and Company, grocers in the Causeway and George Miles a hairdresser. Early closing day was Wednesday. Among other trades listed was Hezekiah Skilton an umbrella maker, Charles Murkett and William

Worlidge the two chimney sweeps, George Negus the Town Crier and Mary Tewter the midwife.

A shop that has played an important role in the town in the recent past is the One Stop Shop. This was once a grocer's shop run by Eddie Ward who originated from London's East End. The shop had many idiosyncrasies including a mynah bird which used to entertain customers despite the strong disapproval of the health inspector. Eddie would make grocery deliveries to the people of Godmanchester in an old mobile library van that he obtained from the former county council.

Transport

The River Great Ouse

The Great Ouse forms the northern boundary of the parish. It is the fourth longest river in the United Kingdom and its source rises close to Brackley in Northamptonshire. The river flows for 150 miles through Bedford, Godmanchester, Earith, and Kings Lynn to the Wash. The Great Ouse has been important to Godmanchester throughout its history as it was a cost effective way of transporting goods. The cost of conveying heavy goods by road was prohibitive. In 1615, sluices were constructed between St Neots and St Ives enabling boats to pass more easily and facilitating the export of grain.[144] Local historian Mary Carter analysed the toll book of Hemingford sluice for 1710 and this revealed that wheat, barley, fish and freestone were regularly being conveyed up river to Bedford. Pots were taken to Tempsford, fish to Wyboston, oats and malt to St Neots, turves to Eaton and pots to Godmanchester. Goods going downstream were malt and wood.[145]

A bridge has connected Godmanchester to Huntingdon for centuries. Edward the Elder built a wooden bridge in the 10th century. At the time of Magna Carta (1215) a major bridge building programme was taking place throughout England and hundreds of new stone bridges were replacing wooden bridges. Such was its impact that Clause 23 of Magna Carta sought to regulate it, 'No vill or man shall be forced to build bridges at river banks, except those who ought to do so by custom and law'.[146] The present stone bridge was built in the 14th century. It replaced a previous bridge destroyed by a storm in 1293. The bridge has six spans and closer examination reveals that it was built by two authorities. It joined over the third pier from the north where a cross marks the boundaries of the two boroughs, Huntingdon and Godmanchester.[147]

Building a stone bridge in the fourteenth century was a pious act. It was something done for other people and in many cases the church granted indulgences for those who built and maintained bridges. It is therefore appropriate that many bridges had chapels built on them.[148] A medieval chapel dedicated to St Thomas Becket and St Katherine once stood on the Godmanchester to Huntingdon bridge but no remains of this chapel survive. Mass was celebrated daily in the chapel and the chaplain was supported by the alms of those crossing the river.[149] Bridge chapels were built at a number of crossings of the River Ouse. As well as the surviving chapel of St Leger at St Ives there were chapels at Bromham, Turvey and Bedford.[150]

Roads

Godmanchester's origins were largely dependent on its location at both the river crossing and the major Roman roads from London to York and Cambridge to Leicester. These major through roads were in constant use. Use of the word 'road' prior to the early modern period is something of an historical anachronism because the contemporary term in the medieval period was 'highway'. Major roads were known as the 'king's highway' and the king regularly travelled on them. If the king found major roads impassable the local manorial lord responsible for its maintenance would quickly hear of it. Local roads were not so well maintained and manorial court records frequently refer to local roads becoming impassable. In the Middle Ages, many people travelled along England's roads. Edward III managed the incredible speed of fifty five miles a day when travelling to York in 1336.[151] Typically travellers completed about twenty miles a day but distances achieved by pack horses varied according to the loads they were carrying. Those riding a horse would not accomplish much greater daily distances unless they had a change of horse.

The first highways act, the Statute for Mending of Highways of 1555 represented the beginning of state control of roads. Each parish in England became responsible for the upkeep of its roads. Like the Poor Law it was another example of devolution of responsibility to the parish. Two unpaid

Surveyors of Highways were elected each year and labour for roads was supplied by parishioners. Anyone with land worth £50 a year, or who kept a draught of horses, supplied two men, a cart and horses and oxen for six days. Everyone else supplied one man or did the work themselves. Gradually the system of supplying labour changed into a money payment. The 1555 Act was not wholly successful as roads required frequent repair but they were not always carried out.

The condition of roads in the seventeenth century is debated. The poor quality of roads has often been inferred from the writings of contemporaries. For example, Daniel Defoe described the road between Biggleswade and Buckden as 'a most frightful way' in 1724. Travellers often turned off it into private land to avoid 'sloughs and holes which no horse could wade through'. However, the historian Christopher Dyer argued that roads were often of a higher quality in the Middle Ages but deteriorated in the seventeenth century as more and heavier vehicles were introduced. Dyer suggested that some criticisms of roads were part of 'the rhetoric of improvement' to convince investors that new roads were required.[152]

The construction of improved roads required replacing piecemeal maintenance by individual parishes with an organisation based on larger areas. Through routes had always been a bone of contention because parishes did not feel they were getting the benefit which largely accrued to carriers and coach owners. Responsibility for through routes was given to Turnpike Trusts. Trustees were typically local landowners and merchants with a direct interest in the improvement of roads.[153] Turnpike Trusts raised capital by loans to repair and build roads and the loans were repaid from tolls. The first Turnpike Act (1663) provided for repairing roads in Hertfordshire, Cambridgeshire and Huntingdonshire.[154] Through roads linked Huntingdon, Godmanchester and St Ives to London and north to King's Lynn through Ramsey.[155]

Turnpike Commissioners were made responsible for the road from Huntingdon into Godmanchester in 1710. Tolls were collected at toll gates and a toll cottage survives in the Avenue.

Toll cottage The Avenue

The road passes over the meadows and Back River by a causeway, which predates 1279 when it was repaired. Robert Cook rebuilt it in 1637 as a thank-offering for his escape from drowning.[156] A stone in the parapet of the southern of the two bridges bears the inscription, *'Robertus Cooke ex aquis emersus hoc viatoribus sacrum D.D. 1637.'* At the end of the eighteenth century, the causeway was enlarged with two series of eight arches allowing the passage of flood water. F. W. Bird recalls that the Black Bull did a thriving trade from farmers and others travelling into Huntingdon for the market. In order to avoid paying the toll, they would put their traps up at the Black Bull and then walk into Huntingdon.[157]

London grew rapidly during the early modern period from about 200,000 people in 1600 to 575,000 in 1700 and almost a million by 1800. The growth of London was fuelled by migration from rural England including many people from Huntingdonshire. This growth created a significantly increased demand for food and raw materials.[158] Roads facilitated Huntingdonshire's contribution to providing food for the capital. The new turnpike roads reduced travelling time and the transport costs of moving freight. They acted as a significant stimulus to economic growth and were one of many factors which explain why England was the first to industrialise.[159]

By the nineteenth century, several coach services ran from Huntingdon to Birmingham, Boston, Cambridge, Edinburgh, Leicester, Newcastle and Stamford. The Edinburgh service called at Stamford, Grantham, Newark, Doncaster, York, Easingwold, Northallerton, Darlington and Durham on route. The two main posting inns in Huntingdon were The George and the Fountain. The George is now the George Hotel and the Fountain is now the '99p Shop' in the Market Square (formerly Woolworths). Four coaches a day left the George for London: The Regent at 10 a.m., the Perseverance at noon, The Boston Mail at 10 p.m. and the Wellington at 10.30 p.m. Mail coaches to Boston and Edinburgh left the Fountain at 4 a.m.[160] The Monarch coach ran from the Horse Shoe Inn in Godmanchester to London every Monday, Wednesday and Friday. Several carrier services also ran to London, Cambridge, Kimbolton, Peterborough, Ramsey, St Ives, St Neots and Stamford.[161]

The coming of the railways marked the beginning of the rapid decline of the turnpike trusts. Their income plummeted and in the second half of the nineteenth century they were increasingly wound up. What had begun as a spur to efficiency was increasingly seen as an intrusion on the liberty of individuals who resented paying tolls. In 1888 the Local Government Act finally transferred responsibility for maintaining main roads to county councils and county borough councils.

Railways

The railways came to Godmanchester in 1847. The Ely and Huntingdon railway opened a line from St Ives to Godmanchester at a cost of £120,000.[162] The original intention was that the railway would continue to Huntingdon but because of a funding shortage it was only went as far as Godmanchester. Godmanchester station opened on 17 August 1847. The station was originally called Huntingdon but was subsequently renamed Godmanchester to avoid confusion with the new GNR Huntingdon station to which trains arrived from London. The East Coast main line from King's Cross to Peterborough line opened in 1850. By contrast, the earlier line to St Ives was just over four miles long and only light locomotives could be used due to the weak wooden bridges.[163] It was an economic disaster from its earliest days and Bob Burn-Murdoch curator of the Norris Museum tells the story of its beginnings. So few passengers used the line that trains stopped running after two years and it was decided to run services comprised of a single carriage pulled by a horse. However, the law required passenger trains to travel at a minimum 12 mph and the poor horse could not aspire to this speed. Train services were resumed in 1850 when the route was extended to Huntingdon.[164]

Virginia Woolf's diary provides an insight into travel by train in 1899. She writes:

> Our journey from Warboys to Huntingdon is one of those infrequent train journeys ...which are a splendid triumph for the bicycle. You can bicycle with comfort and pleasure into Huntingdon [in] under an hour. It takes just the same to do the 8 miles in the train...with two changes at Somersham and St Ives.

Virginia was on her way to Godmanchester where her uncle and cousins lived. She had great problems with the trains, missed the connection at St Ives and finished up taking a pony and trap.[165]

The railways were nationalised in 1948 and seven trains ran between Godmanchester and St Ives six days a week. However, the service only lasted another eleven years and the line closed to passengers in 1959 and to freight in 1962. The site of the station today is Huntingdonshire District Council's Car Park, adjacent to RGE Engineering.[166] All that can still be seen is the Crossing Keeper's house directly opposite the car park and part of the former railway trackway which now forms part of the Ouse Valley Way footpath towards St Ives.

Former Railway Bridge crossing the river at Huntingdon

Journey times dramatically reduced during the twentieth century. In 1905 it took two hours to travel from London Kings Cross. By 1982, the journey time had fallen to just 39 minutes as the last stop for the 125 express train coming from the north was Huntingdon. The disadvantage of this arrangement was the difficulty of obtaining a seat during peak hours. The electrification of the railway led to slightly longer journey times so that the fastest train to London is now 50 minutes.

The Motor Car

Just as the coming of the railways spelled the demise of turnpike trusts so the motor car threatened the success of railways. But the dominance of the motor car took some time to arrive. The Motor Car Act passed in 1903 raised the speed limit from 12 to 20 mph and required cars to be registered with number plates. Although the Act introduced driving licences there was no driving test. Just 17,000 cars were registered in Britain immediately following the Act. The first person to own a car in Godmanchester was Violet Beart of Island Hall.

The introduction of the motor car led to a spate of accidents. Despite the fact that there were only 140,000 cars on the road there were no less than 145,000 accidents in the country in 1910.[167] Godmanchester was no exception. In 1905, *The Hunts Post* reported that Mr E. Deighton was driving through West Street when the wheel of his vehicle came off. Fortunately nobody was hurt.[168] An accident involving a 40 H.P. Landaulette belonging to the London Taximeter company between Lattenbury Hill and Kisby's Hut in 1908 was more serious. The driver endeavouring to avoid a perambulator skidded, crashed through a hedge and turned over. Fortunately the driver managed to crawl out and make his way back to Godmanchester.[169] In 1909 John White, Headmaster of the Boys National School in Huntingdon, was travelling with the proprietor of the Fountain Hotel. Mr Darke the driver skidded and crashed into the lamp post opposite the White Hart Public House in Godmanchester. Mr White was thrown out of the car and 'laid helpless' on the ground. Dr Combe was called and the shaken Mr White was driven back to his house where he was confined to bed for a couple of days.[170]

Accidents were not confined to the newly arrived motor car. The following year *The Hunts Post* reported that 'several people had narrow escapes from serious injury' when a horse escaped in London Street. Mr Walker a Godmanchester farmer was preparing to drive out in his horse and trap with his wife. Sidney George was harnessing the horse to the trap but omitted to take off the halter. He removed the bridle to get the halter off but Mrs Walker was not holding the reins and the fresh horse bolted. It made straight for a cottage between the Plough and Golden Lion public houses. It crashed into the cottage, knocking off the door and demolishing a considerable part of the front wall. The occupant Mrs Clifton a widow was having tea and unsurprisingly suffered 'severe shock'. Mrs Walker, the farmer's wife was still in the trap but managed to get out and 'took refuge in the house of Miss Bester'. Mrs Walker was badly bruised and dazed and Mrs Clifton's room was 'a complete wreck' and her furniture and pictures were smashed.

Businesses geared up for the motor car. For example, the Old Bridge Hotel advertised itself as a first class residential and touring hotel. Its facilities included smoking, card and billiard rooms and meals served at all hours to motorists.[171]

Today the motor car reigns supreme. More than three quarters of Godmanchester residents now own at least one car and 70 per cent travel to work by car or motor cycle. Only seven per cent go to work by either bus or train.[172] However, the massive growth of car ownership has resulted in clogged roads. The A14 has frequently been described as 'the road to hell' rather than to Cambridge and beyond. In 2004, listeners to BBC Radio Cambridgeshire voted for suitable music to relieve the tension and stress of driving along the A14. The top three A14 anthems voted for by listeners were:

> Chris Rea - Road to Hell;
> Louis Armstrong - We Have All The Time in the World;
> Talking Heads - Road to Nowhere.

The much delayed 'Guided Bus' is seen as the solution by some but it is too early to make a judgement at the time of writing.

Recent Economic Trends

Geography continues to be the key to Godmanchester's more recent economy. Located next to the A14, the town is ideally placed to provide distribution services for goods. At Cardinal Distribution Park, Wincanton Distribution for Somerfield and D.H.L. Logistics are to be found. New industries have arrived in Godmanchester such as Comtec Cable Accessories which provides services to the communications industry.

Employment patterns have also changed markedly over the last twenty five years. Although the percentage of adult men in employment has steadily declined, the percentage of economically active women has grown. Three quarters of all adult females including no less than 43 per cent of women with children under five years old now work. This has led to an increasing demand for day nursery places and playgroups.

7

RELIGION

The first appearance of religious practice was when humans began disposing of their dead in a ceremonial manner. This seems to indicate at least a journey into an afterlife but not necessarily belief in divine beings.[173] Attempts to date the earliest examples of rituals associated with burial are fraught with difficulty because the intentional nature of such rituals is difficult to prove. For example, was the placing of flowers on a corpse an example of ritual or an attempt to ameliorate the smell?[174] One very early example of possible ritual practice relates to the Herto people, a group of *homo sapiens* in Africa dating back 160,000 years. The Herto removed heads from corpses shortly after death. Cut marks near the base of their skulls have been interpreted as a ritual practice.[175] Carl Zimmer argues that modern man was carefully burying their dead in caves 130,000 years ago.[176] Sheila Coulson claims to have discovered mankind's oldest known ritual in Botswana. According to the San peoples' creation myth, mankind descended from the python. Coulson believes that a cave in Tsodila Hills, Botswana was the centre of ritual activity devoted to the python. She found over 300 man-made indentations in the cave depicting a python. The 'tools' interpreted as used for creating the depictions are dated to approximately 70,000 years ago.[177]

The earliest evidence of religious activity in Godmanchester was much more recent! It took place at a Neolithic temple built some 5,000 years ago. The temple's 24 wooden obelisks were aligned with the lunar and solar cycles but the main focus of the alignment is with sunrise on May 1st (Beltane) and August 1st (Lugnasad). Religious festivals were aligned to the agricultural year. Beltane was the midpoint between the spring equinox and summer solstice and marked the beginning of the summer season when livestock was driven out to the summer pastures. Lugnasad, associated with the later Iron Age deity Lugh, celebrated the beginning of the harvest season.

Iron Age people worshipped both general and local deities. Godmanchester had its own god, Abandinus known from a single inscription on a bronze votive feather found in the town:

> *"To the god Abandinus Vatiaucus gave this from his own resources'.*[178]

The inscribed feather was one of a number found close to one of the Roman Temples by Michael Green in 1971. Michael Green described the event when 'a ball of rolled-up stuff fell into my hand. When the bronze sheets were unrolled the inscribed feather was revealed'. Nothing is known about this god but the etymology of the word suggests associations with water or a river. 'Aban' is believed to be a variant of Avon, a Celtic word meaning river. The association of deities with water was common in the Iron Age period. Offerings at river crossings have led to some spectacular discoveries such as the shields from Witham and Battersea which are proudly displayed at the British Museum. The origins of Godmanchester are linked to its strategic importance as a river crossing and therefore it is appropriate that it is linked with a river god.

Roman Godmanchester had two Temples. The first is known as the Temple of Abandinus and is located just to the west of the *mansio* under present-day Granary Close on the north side of the west to east road through the Roman town. The temple was interpreted by Michael Green as the Temple of Abandinus as a result of finding the inscribed votive feather.

Three successive temples were built on the Granary Close site. The earliest temple dates from the early second century and was a simple rectangular building measuring about 5m by 7m. The much improved second version was made of wood and was carried on a timber framework of uprights. This temple was probably destroyed during the fire of 296 when the mansio complex was destroyed. The third version built in the fourth century had a polygonal rather than a rectangular plan. In the centre of the third version of the temple Greene found a masonry tank which he interpreted as further evidence of association with a water deity. Reconstructions of the second and third versions of the temple are shown in the illustration by Michael Green. A second temple in Pipers Lane was not attributed to any deity. It was found about 100 meters into the town after you entered by the South

Gate. The building was demolished in the fourth century and replaced by a timber shop.

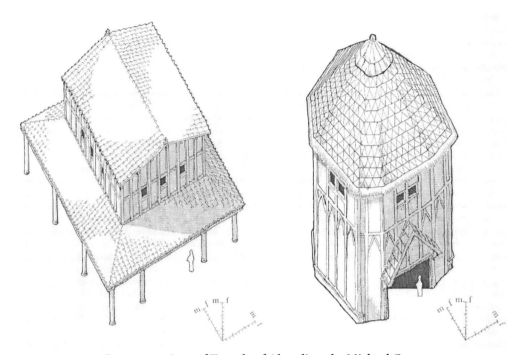

Reconstructions of Temple of Abandinus by Michael Green

Classical gods were worshipped in Godmanchester and the surrounding area. The most popular god appears to be Mercury, as figurines depicting him have been found not just in Godmanchester but also Fenstanton and Cambridge.[179] Like the Greek god Hermes, Mercury was an economic god, who looked after the movement of goods, particularly grain. He had close links with shopkeepers and the transporters of goods.[180]

Venus, the Roman goddess of love, was also popular. A pottery model of Venus found near the *Mansio* in Godmanchester was made in France about AD 150.[181]

Venus the Goddess of love
(Norris Museum, St Ives)

A recent excavation at 8 New Street, Godmanchester led to the discovery of a copper alloy handle with a 'zoomorphic terminal' which may have been a votive offering. The animal depicted has not been determined but could be a crocodile. Objects which depict crocodiles are very rare in Roman Britain. The crocodile's association with water would make it an appropriate offering to the town's river god, Abandinus.[182]

Christianity did not arrive in England with St Augustine in 597. The Emperor Constantine's conversion led to Christianity becoming the official religion of the Roman Empire and the Edict of Milan in 313 granted to Christians 'full authority to observe their religion'. Only a year later in 314, three British bishops from London, York and Lincoln attended the Council of Arles in France to discuss the heresy of Donatism.[183] This suggests that the Christian church was established throughout England prior to Constantine's conversion. However, Christian church buildings relating to the Roman period are very difficult to identify particularly in more rural areas. Most were built of wood and no traces have survived. One exception is a simple rectangular building uncovered at Icklingham in Suffolk. The clues to it being used for Christian purposes are the associated lead tanks which were inscribed with a monogram comprising the two Greek letters *chi* (X) and *rho* (P), the first two letters of the title, Christ (χριστος). These were undoubtedly baptismal fonts. Surrounding the building were over 40 burials with their heads to the west.[184]

Huntingdonshire provided further evidence of early Christianity when an important discovery was made at Water Newton (*Durobrivae*) near Peterborough in 1975. A hoard of Roman silver dating from the 4th century included many objects with the *chi-rho* (XP) monogram and also the Greek letters alpha and omega, references to Christ as the first and the last. This find represents the earliest group of Christian liturgical silver found in the entire Roman Empire and they are now on display in the British Museum. Lead tanks which were used as early baptism fonts have also been found in a number of locations including Huntingdon and Willingham, Cambridgeshire.[185]

Although England was part of the officially Christian Roman Empire, in much of the country it was still probably a minority religion. The polytheism of the Iron Age remained and pagan practice was strong particularly in the countryside.[186] The collapse of Roman rule in Britain therefore raised serious questions about whether Christianity would survive. There was a resurgence of pagan belief and the arrival of Anglo-Saxons further strengthened paganism particularly in the east of the country where these new immigrants first settled. Augustine's mission which led to the reconversion of Britain is well documented and by the seventh century the Christian Church had triumphed.

St Mary's Parish Church

The earliest Christian church in Godmanchester was probably wooden and likely to have been built on the site of the present church, the highest point in the old town. The second church was also probably made of wood. Most churches were wooden in the Saxon period although there are some notable local exceptions at Brixworth and Earls Barton. Godmanchester church is recorded in Domesday Book (1086) but little information is given, a mere five words, 'a priest and a church'.[187] However, some idea of wooden churches in this period might be gleaned from a visit to the church of St Andrew at Greensted-juxta-Ongar approximately ten miles from Epping. St Andrews is thought to be the oldest surviving wooden church in England. Tree-ring dating suggests that its wooden nave walls date from the eleventh century.

St Mary's Church

St Mary's Godmanchester may have been a Minster Church.[188] Before the development of parish churches Anglo-Saxon minster churches functioned as religious communities from which preachers went out to surrounding communities. Colin Platt explains them well, 'Under the patronage of king and bishop, minster clergy carried the word of God out into the estates and villages, offering the facilities of a central church for baptism and burial or for the observance by a large congregation of the more important of the Christian festivals'.[189]

Godmanchester Church initially belonged to Ramsey Abbey. Ramsey Abbey was founded in 969 by Oswald and Æthelwine. Several monasteries were established in the Fenland in the tenth century as it was an excellent place to withdraw from the world. Ramsey Abbey was provided with estates throughout Huntingdonshire. One of the churches given to the new Abbey was Godmanchester, a gift from King Edgar (959-75). In the twelfth century, King Stephen (1135-54) gave Godmanchester church and its associated land to Merton Priory. The Prior of Merton had a manor house to the east of Godmanchester Church. The house is shown on a map of 1524 which depicts a substantial complex of one and two-storey buildings with tiled roofs and ornate chimneys. The house is believed to have been demolished soon after Merton Priory was dissolved in 1538. The moated site where the Prior's house originally stood is now a scheduled monument.[190]

Merton Priory in Surrey was an important monastic house. According to Matthew Paris, Merton Priory was founded around 1117 when the first canons came to Merton from Huntingdon's Augustinian Priory. Their leader was Alwin, the sub-prior of the Augustinian Priory. Alwin subsequently became King David of Scotland's chaplain and when King David wished to house the 'fragment of the Holy Cross' his mother had brought from the Holy Land in 1128 he invited Alwin and other Merton canons to set up a monastery in Edinburgh. The monastery became Holyrood Abbey and Alwin was the first abbot. All that remains of Merton Priory today are the foundations of the chapter house. The site was excavated between 1976 and 1990 and many artefacts were discovered.[191]

Godmanchester church was built in the Perpendicular Style. The oldest part of the present building is in the chancel and dates from the thirteenth century. The octagonal font is also thirteenth century. About 1340 a north vestry was added to the chancel, and subsequently further reconstruction took place at the west end of the aisles and including the arcades, clerestory and porches. The chancel was also raised and altered. The fifteenth century choir stalls were designed to support frail or elderly monks who had to stand for long periods of time during services. Pevsner considered the impressive misericords under the stalls to be 'the best in the former county'.[192] The animals depicted include a fox carrying a goose in his mouth and a cat holding a mouse. Lloyd considers them indigenous to the church but Wickes argues that they probably came from Ramsey Abbey.[193]

The Black Death had a dramatic effect on the church which lost half its clergy in twelve months. In Huntingdonshire there were no less than 79 clergy installed to vacant benefices in 1349 compared to 15 in 1348.[194] Those who died of the pestilence included the Prior of Huntingdon and the Prioress of Hinchingbrooke. When their services were most in demand, priests were increasingly scarce. People who feared death without the administration of the last rites were thrown unconfessed into plague pits. Just as the remaining labourers sought higher wages so too did the few remaining clergy who demanded massively increased stipends.

Prior to the Reformation, fear of the pains of purgatory loomed large in the hearts of lay people as they approached death. Whilst all Christians might hope to go to heaven, only 'saints' were admitted to heaven immediately. Ordinary souls must first suffer physical torment to prepare them for heaven. The medieval mind was preoccupied with the need to ensure that souls passed safely from this world to the next. Whereas we might see the process of making a will being chiefly about what happens to our assets after death, to the medieval mind it was principally a religious document preparing souls for the afterlife. Spiritual and material debts left undischarged would result in a longer period in purgatory.[195] So the soon to be deceased required that 'tithes and offerings negligently forgotten' should be paid by his executors. Even more important were payments for masses to be sung to aid the release of the soul from purgatory. The fate of those in purgatory could be affected by the prayers of the living as they could reduce the time the dead would spend in purgatory. To ensure that prayers were said for them after their death, many rich people left vast amounts of money to endow chantries.

Chantries were foundations, where priests were employed to say masses for the souls of their founders in perpetuity. Although varying in form, chantries were literally places where a priest would chant masses for the dead, often on the anniversary of a person's death. A chantry priest could be funded full time out of a person's estate. Their duties could be stipulated by the deceased person and these might include celebrating mass and regularly saying prayers for the person's soul. The employment of a full-time chaplain would cost from five or six marks per annum up to about six pounds. A mark was two thirds of a pound and therefore these sums are the equivalent of from ten to eighteen labourers' wages for a year. As inflation increased so the support of chantry priests became increasingly difficult to fund. Some wills recognised this and accepted that the priests might revert to part-time duties. An alternative was to restrict the term of the priest's duties to a limited time period, say twenty years.[196] Henry VIII died shortly after the passing of the first Chantries Act and it was left to his son Edward VI to suppress the chantries. Chantries and their properties passed to the king. Many chantries were converted into grammar schools but the great wealth which accrued to the crown was used to wage war on France.

Very few people could afford to endow a chantry priest. Guilds operated collectively and organised prayers for the souls of deceased brothers. Guilds organised devotional activities such as maintenance of lights for particular altars or statues in church and practiced charitable activity. They came more into fashion after the Black Death. Eight guilds and chantries are recorded in the Godmanchester sources. The chantry of St Mary dates back at least as far as the reign of Edward I and Roode's chantry was in existence in 1297 when Martin was the chaplain. Corpus Christi was begun 'by the devotion of parishioners to have a priest sing mass' and Corpus Christi Lane is named after it.[197] The guild of St John the Baptist had an altar and statue in St Mary's church and the remaining were dedicated to the Holy Trinity, St Catherine, St George and St James.

In 1264 Pope Urban IV founded the Feast of Corpus Christi and this culminated in the solemn procession of the Blessed Sacrament. Members of a Corpus Christi guild might provide funds for torches to be carried during the procession. Many guilds celebrated a common meal for its members. These meals were the most important event in the guild's calendar. Some guilds had their own stock of tableware for these occasions and their tableware such as pewter plates would often include the guild insignia. It was a common practice for members of guilds to leave bequests to their guild and such bequests appear in a number of Godmanchester wills. Thomas Robyns left half a quarter of barley each to the Guilds of St John the Baptist and Corpus Christi in his will of 1306.[198] In 1483, Agnes Lane left half an acre of meadow to the Guild of the Holy Trinity and in 1491 Thomas Froste left half an acre of meadow to the Guild of Corpus Christi.[199]

Corpus Christi Lane

The Reformation had an enormous impact on religious activity in Godmanchester as elsewhere. The Priory of Merton was dissolved in 1538 and Godmanchester church granted to the Dean and Chapter of Westminster. The control of the church was probably of less importance to the laity than changes in religious belief imposed from above. In 1536, 'images' that were sacrificed to and therefore now considered idolatrous were to be taken down 'forthwith'. Lights before the rood screen and by the sepulchre were still allowed to burn but in 1541 these too were banned and the only permitted light was for the altar. In 1545 and 1547, purgatory was abolished and chantries and guilds swept away.

In 1623 the church tower collapsed. What remained of the tower was taken down and rebuilt in the same perpendicular gothic style. Much of the old stone from the original thirteenth-century building was used.[200] In order to pay for the rebuilding of the tower, a levy was imposed on the people of Godmanchester: 12*d* for every acre of meadow, 4*d* for every acre of arable land and layes and the several enclosures and pigstels about the town.

The document setting out the levy has survived. The levy was made to take down the 'shattered and decayed steeple and breach and rebuilding again the same & repair of the church to the honour of almightie God & Christian religion'.

A levy for rebuilding the tower (Huntingdonshire Archives)[201]

The church has been continually restored up to the present day. The upper part of the south porch was rebuilt around 1669. Major changes were made to the church while Charles Gray was Vicar. In 1853, the reseating of the church and restoring the towers cost no less than £800. Only two years later in 1855 the new East window cost a further £350. In 1859, a new organ built by Bryceson of London was installed at a total cost of £500.[202]

An important primary source for church alterations is Churchwardens' account books. Unfortunately, with the exception of two pages for the sixteenth century, these only survive in Godmanchester for the period after 1813.[203] One of the sixteenth-century pages includes details of wages paid to Richard and John Garlope for three and a half days work each revealing that the rate of pay was 8d a day. John Burrowe and his boy were paid 11d a day for four days work suggesting that a boys wage was 3d. An undated page records payments for carrying the communion table (not an altar) and for the bible indicating that the Reformation had already taken place. Nineteenth-century accounts detail regular payments for such items as candles, washing robes and mending surplices. Annual wages paid to bell ringers and singers in church are recorded and also intermittent payments for shovelling snow from the church. Although, major improvements to the church fabric are listed they are frustratingly bereft of detail. Exceptions were repairs to the church clock at £23 in 1838 and the new church gates which cost £30 13s in 1852. The Church Rate to finance this expenditure was set each year and was usually 2d or 3d in the pound. When major repairs were required this rate was substantially increased; for example, to one shilling in the pound in 1832. For many years in the late Victorian period a Mrs Boot was paid three shillings and six pence (17.5p) each week for cleaning in the church. In 1900 payments for a church organist started to appear. Mr Horley's salary was set at £15 per annum but had increased to £20 a year by 1915 when the organist was a Mr Wybray.

In 1901, Bodley designed the gilt wood carving and figures of the high altar of the reredos. The erection of the reredos and screen in the church was a gift of the Bevan family. It was controversial and incurred criticism from some people in the town. Martin Travers (1886-1948), an architect and stained glass artist, designed the St Anne's altar and reredos at the east end of the south aisle in 1937. The carved wood reredos is a 'linen fold' design with the text from St Luke, 'HE HATH VISITED AND REDEEMED HIS PEOPLE'. The altar and reredos were given in memory of Iona Mary Tillard and her son Philip and serve as a memorial to the Baumgartner and Tillard families. By the altar is a sculpture of St Anne with the Virgin Mary, made by John Fox, a Godmanchester craftsman.

There are three striking windows in the south aisle of the church commemorating the Baumgartners and the Tillards. The window, in memory of General Baumgartner (1814-1895) was designed by William Morris and Company.[204] Christ with two angels is depicted at the top of the window and the lower figures represent justice, courage and humility. Two other windows are dedicated to the Tillard family: the nativity to Philippa and the modified 'Jesse window' to her husband Philip.

The historic fabric of the building requires increasing amounts of money to be raised. In the last thirty years significant sums have been spent including the restoration of the heating system and the Bryceson organ. The ceremony to celebrate the completion of the organ restoration was attended by Dames Norma Major and Emily Blatch. Not all of the effort of the church is put into raising money for the building. The church would place the regular acts of worship on Sundays as its priority. Godmanchester Church has twice featured in the long running BBC television programme *Songs of Praise*. The show is one of the longest running TV series and dates back to 1961. The programme on Godmanchester in 1975 was a milestone for the series in being the first to include interviews. When the programme returned to the town one of the interviewees was Mary Hardy who had appeared in the first programme. The former primary school teacher spoke movingly of the passing of a whole Godmanchester generation since the first programme had been filmed.

The Churchyard

The churchyard has much to reveal about the history of Godmanchester. The south wall of the chancel is the earliest surviving part of the church building and dates from the thirteenth century. A mass dial is built on a buttress of the chancel wall.

The mass was the most important element of worship in the medieval period. In the sacrifice of the mass, Christ became present in every parish church in the land. The belief in transubstantiation meant that in the Eucharist Christ's body and blood were literally consumed. The priest would say mass daily but the common man would only attend on Sunday and at festivals. The time of mass was indicated on a mass dial. Medieval mass dials came in a variety of designs and sizes; from semi-circles of dots to complete circles with their radii. Two mass dials in Gloucestershire, where the survival of mass dials is relatively common, range from only 70mm. diameter at Boddington to 400mm. at Leckhampton. Mass dials are usually found on the south wall of the church as in Godmanchester,

Godmanchester's Mass Dial

The well-known tombstone of Mary Weems is also on the south side of the church adjacent to the path. The tragic story of Mary and Thomas Weems is recounted on the tombstone. Mary Weems (nee Dixon) got to know Thomas Weems of Godmanchester and they were married at Goldington Church, Bedfordshire. The marriage was not a happy one and

Thomas left Mary and went to live in London. Thomas found himself another woman, Mary Woodward and wanted to marry her but his legal wife stood in his way. Pretending to be reconciled to Mary, Thomas Weems invited her to travel with him to London and murdered her on the way at Wendy in 1819. Thomas was arrested and held in Cambridge Gaol, the site of Shire Hall.[205] Thomas was found guilty at his trial and hanged.

The transcription of the text of Mary's tombstone reads:

To the Young of both Sexes

This Stone is erected by public Subscription over the remains of MARY ANN WEEMS who at an early age became acquainted with THOMAS WEEMS formerly of this Parish this connextion [sic] terminating in a compulsory Marriage occasioned him soon to desert her and wishing to be Married to another Woman he filled up the measure of his iniquity by resolving to murder his Wife which he barbarously perpetrated at Wendy on their Journey to London toward which place he had induced her to go under the mask of reconciliation May the 7th 1819 He was taken within a few hours after the crime was committed, tried and subsequently executed at Cambridge on the 7th of August in the same Year

Ere Crime you perpetrate survey this Stone Learn hence the God of Justice sleeps not on his Throne But marks the Sinner with unerring Eye The suffering Victim hears and makes the Guilty die

The original memorial was smashed in 1967 while a nearby tree was being lopped and the present stone is a replacement.

Mary Weems Tombstone 1

Mary Weems Tombstone 2

Funerals

A deeper appreciation of funeral rituals aids our understanding of the churchyard. When writing Martin Chuzzlewit in 1843, Charles Dickens posed the question, 'Why do people spend more money upon a death, Mrs Gump, than upon a birth?' he was reflecting a trend that was common in the previous two centuries.

The costs of funeral rituals are recorded in two important surviving sources: probate accounts and overseers of the poor accounts. The mean cost of a Huntingdonshire funeral recorded in 249 probate accounts in the quarter century 1675-1700 was £5 and the median £3. The cost of individual funerals ranged widely from just seven shillings and six pence to £106 in Huntingdonshire. The most striking feature of funeral costs recorded in probate accounts was the amount of money spent on food and drink.[206] It commonly amounted to half the cost of burying someone and could be as much as three quarters or more of total costs.[207] Food and drink amounted to more than half the total cost of burying someone in over two thirds of Huntingdonshire probate accounts. Mourners were commonly fortified with beer, wine or spirits and they expected food and drink commensurate with the deceased's social rank.[208] A barber from Godmanchester, John Dickenson, had goods worth £47 15s when he died in 1676. His funeral cost over £6, more than the funeral expenditure of half the gentry whose records survive. Two thirds of the cost of Dickenson's funeral was spent on food and drink; bread and cakes at £2 10s and a hogshead of beer for £1 12s 6d. The Overseers of the Poor accounts for Godmanchester show that beer was provided for mourners even at paupers' funerals.

The elite tried to distinguish themselves from the masses. People could be buried in the most expensive lead coffins or their shrouded body might be placed in a reusable parish coffin for the duration of the funeral ceremony. Clare Gittings suggested that poorer people would at least be carried to the grave in the communal coffin and then the body was buried just in its shroud. However, most Huntingdonshire probate accounts included expenditure on a coffin and the median value of Huntingdonshire coffins in the late seventeenth century was ten shillings. An excavation of a Quaker burial ground in 2006 at Hemingford Grey showed that use of coffins was widespread.[209] Overseers of the Poor accounts in Great Gransden recorded a coffin costing 10 shillings which was provided for 'an old beggar man found dead under a haycock' in 1680.[210] Overseers of the Poor in both Godmanchester and Kimbolton also provided coffins for a number of pauper funerals.[211] In Godmanchester, the price of seven coffins for paupers in the three year period 1787-89 was lower than comparative prices for those recorded in probate accounts. Five coffins cost nine shillings and the other two cost six shillings.

Parish bells tolled when a person was dying and rang again when the funeral service took place. Tolling the bell was variously interpreted by Protestant and Catholic but after the restoration of the monarchy in 1660 it symbolised the rehabilitation of the ceremonies of the Church of England. In 1789, Overseers of the Poor in Godmanchester provided beer costing 3s and 2s 10d for the toll bearers at the funerals of John Ray and a deceased person recorded as Bright.

Funeral sermons became more common from the seventeenth century onwards and followed a set pattern.[212] A text would be expounded to remind mourners of their own mortality and this would be followed by a biography of the deceased. Ralph Houlbrooke suggested that the description of the deceased's character was awaited with keenest anticipation. The preacher carefully selected what was good from the person's life and drew a veil over the rest. In this way he could both satisfy the expectations of the congregation and his own conscience.[213] Income from funeral sermons at ten shillings per funeral was a lucrative business for clergymen.

Washing, winding and watching were all involved in preparing the body for burial. Neighbouring women and female servants were frequently employed to clean and dress a corpse.[214] Winding the corpse in a sheet or burial shroud was the minimum requirement for a decent burial for only animals were buried naked. Legislation in 1678 required all bodies to be buried in wool in order to support the domestic woollen industry.[215] This is reflected in a number of payments in probate accounts where woollen cloth is expressly recorded. The custom of sitting up all night watching the body applied to both rich and poor. The intention was to safeguard the body and to ensure that there was somebody present if the corpse revived. In 1720, women were paid 2s 6d for laying out Henry Careless, a waterman from Godmanchester, and a further 3s 6d was paid for watching the body, victuals and drink for the watchers and for the fire and candle.

The second oldest surviving gravestone in Godmanchester churchyard is that of Robert Vinter who died in 1723. It is to be found to the south east of the chancel. The inscription reads, 'Here lyeth the Body of Robert Vinter who dyed February 16th 1723 aged 49.'

Gravestone of Robert Vinter (1723)

Vinter's probate inventory reveals that he was a tailor with moveable goods valued at £34 8s 6d. Although there is no probate account to give details of his funeral it also probably represented a significant proportion of his assets. When Vintner died he was only 49 years old but perhaps saddest of all is that his moveable goods included three barrels of beer in his buttery worth 16 shillings which he had not got round to drinking!

Taking pride of place on the north side of the church is the tombstone of Doctor John Baumgartner and his wife, Philippa.

Doctor John Baumgartner's tomb

The nonconformist burial ground is located in the most northerly part of the churchyard. It is easy to locate because the grass in this part of the churchyard is usually very long. The ownership and hence responsibility for the upkeep of the nonconformist burial ground has been a matter of repeated discussion at the Town Council. For example, the council's minutes in 2007 recorded:

> Mr Sursham had written asking permission to tidy up the nonconform-
> ist burial ground. It was confirmed the Men's Group of the Church PCC
> maintained the main burial ground. It was AGREED that the Town
> Clerk would write to Mr Sursham advising him it was not our (i.e.
> Town Council) land and we could not therefore grant permission.

The result is that the grass is often not cut and these tombstones are often difficult to approach let alone read. But the effort is worthwhile because they contain gems of historical interest. Many contain biblical texts that would not be used on tombstones today. One example is the tomb of Joseph Oldfield the longest serving pastor of the Particular Baptist Church. Oldfield is buried with his two wives. The text from Paul's letter to the church at Rome reads, 'He staggered not at the promises of God through unbelief, but was strong in faith giving glory to God'.

Rev Joseph Oldfield and his tombstone
(Reproduced by permission of Gospel Standard Library)

The nonconformist burial ground

There is a more obvious feature to these tombstones. Parties on historical walks often fail to notice it but obvious features are often easy to miss!

The nonconformist gravestones face north to south whereas the Anglicans are aligned east to west. East-west alignment was the Christian tradition as the deceased faced east from where Christ would reappear at the end of the world.

Nonconformity in Godmanchester

Nonconformity is a relatively recent phenomenon. Prior to the Reformation there was one church in Godmanchester, the Catholic Church. We perhaps need to remind ourselves that St Mary's was that Catholic Church. The term 'nonconformist' was first used to describe those who left the Church of England after the Act of Uniformity in 1662. The earlier term was dissenters used for those who 'either obstinately refuse or wholly absent themselves from the Communion of the Church of England'. Dissenters were not always easy to define for they could be total separatists (mainly Baptists and Quakers) or partial conformists (Presbyterians and Independents) who attended the parish church in the morning but might attend a 'conventicle' in the afternoon.

In 1676 a census of religious adherence was taken. It was overseen by the Bishop of London, Henry Compton, and so is commonly called the 'Compton Census'. Incumbents were required to report total numbers of three groups: Conformists, Popish Recusants and Dissenters. The results purported to show that less than 5 per cent of the population were dissenters although it is likely that many 'partial conformists' who worshipped at both Anglican and dissenter places of worship were counted as Anglicans. The results of the census suggest relatively high numbers of dissenters in Godmanchester. In the Huntingdonshire Hundred of Toseland, just over 5 per cent of the totals recorded by the Compton Census were dissenters but in Godmanchester 65 (8 per cent) were classified dissenters. The epicentre of dissent in the county was Warboys with 18 per cent dissenters.

A second religious census took place in 1851. Russell's Whig government carried out a religious census at the same time as the general census. Its purpose was to find out whether there was sufficient room to accommodate worshippers in the churches and chapels of England. The results were variously interpreted to assess the relative strengths of nonconformity and the established church. The Registrar General employed Horace Mann to carry out the religious census. The census recorded worshippers at the various services on Sunday 30 March 1851 and therefore people who attended more than one service inflated the total.

The results of the census were a shock to many people who assumed that anyone who claimed to be a Christian would visit a place of worship every Sunday.[216] However, the census demonstrated that attendances represented only about half of the population in England. Godmanchester was above average in that attendances (1352) equated to 58 per cent of the total population of 2337. The second shock was that the Anglican Church claimed the allegiance of only about half the practising believers in England and Wales. In Godmanchester 55 per cent of attendances were in the Parish Church but this was mainly due to its large Sunday School. The results of the census were contested nationally and locally. Charles Gray, Vicar of St Mary's, Godmanchester recorded on the census return that he did not consider that attendance figures were a valid measure of the relative position of the Church of England and nonconformity. He argued that 'attendance at meeting by no means necessarily implies conscientious dissent from the church'.[217] However, the four nonconformist chapels in Godmanchester might argue that they were under-represented because their preaching services did not only take place on a Sunday. Both Particular Baptist Chapels did not have preaching services on the nominated Sunday and claimed that attendances were reduced as a result. The results of the census fuelled the animosity between church and nonconformity nationally. The battles were over disestablishment, church rates and education. The nonconformists' numerical strength revealed by the census added weight to their campaign for abolition of church rates, which finally occurred in 1868.

Baptists

Christian denominations were spread very unevenly across the country. The 1851 census revealed that Huntingdonshire was in the centre of the Baptist heartland and so it is no surprise to find that they were so strong in Godmanchester. Nationally their roots go back to the sixteenth century and they divide into two groups: Arminian General Baptists and Calvinistic

Particular Baptists. Both groups were represented in Godmanchester but only one survives today.

Godmanchester Baptist Church

Godmanchester Baptist Church was formerly known as Duck End Chapel, Union Chapel and Silver Street Baptist Church. The Borough Treasurer, Frederick William Bird born in Godmanchester in 1837 recorded in 1911 that he remembered the Baptist Union Chapel being built in Silver Street 'about sixty years ago'.[218] This is broadly consistent with Michael Green's statement that the Chapel was founded in 1844 and the Church's claim that it has been in existence since 1845.[219] Bird wrote that it was erected by Harratt of Huntingdon, who was a worshipper there. Tunmore, the first minister, 'was an eloquent young preacher' who drew large congregations. Frederick Bird reports that two ladies who lived opposite took a lively interest in the proceedings of this chapel and whenever they saw any church people going there they felt it to be their duty to report the matter to the Vicar.[220] The Chapel was rebuilt in 1975. As a result of an expanding congregation the church moved to a disused factory in East Chadley Lane and sold the Silver Street premises to the Salvation Army.

Godmanchester Baptist Church

At the end of 2008 the church had 133 members and its estimated worshipping community was around 200.[221] The Senior Pastor John Smith joined the church in January 2009.

Particular Baptist Church

The Calvinistic Particular Baptists had a thriving church in Cambridge Street in the nineteenth century. All that now remains is a memorial garden containing a number of tombstones.

Particular Baptist Church, now a memorial garden

The land for the Particular Baptist Church was provided in 1796 by Edward Martin who according to Thomas Pack, the chapel's appointed historian, 'exercised great influence'. The first Pastor of the church was Thomas Stevens Freeman. When Freeman arrived in 1813 the church was 'distinctly Arminian...devoid of all knowledge of the principles of grace'. Arminians rejected the doctrines of Calvinism. Arminians believed that Jesus died for all and not just the predestined elect. Furthermore God's grace could be resisted and Christians could fall from grace. Such beliefs were anathema to Calvinists for whom the label Arminian was a term of abuse. Edward Martin was an Arminian who found the Calvinist doctrines of free grace 'obnoxious'. He soon discovered to his horror that the new Pastor, Freeman was a Calvinist.

Freeman won over the majority of the congregation to Calvinism who formed themselves into a Particular Baptist Church. The chapel was built in 1815. Martin and his family left the chapel and campaigned against Freeman. Thomas Pack the chapel's historian was a convinced Calvinist and unsurprisingly strongly sided with Freeman in the dispute. Pack wrote that 'Freeman was assailed in the public streets and hooted in terms of the greatest scurrility and in the most vulgar manner by the lowest orders of society who were aided and abetted by Mr Martin'. However, the dispute was ratcheted up several notches when Freeman formed an attachment with Edward Martin's daughter Eliza who consented to correspond with him. Martin discovered the liaison, accused Pastor Freeman of 'grave moral offences' and threatened to read passages from the correspondence to the whole congregation on the following Sunday! When the church agreed to this suggestion, Martin backtracked, sent his daughter away from Godmanchester and she finally married an Anglican clergyman. Sadly Thomas Freeman died at the age of 35 in 1821, having been the Pastor for just seven years. He was buried together with his sister Fanny in front of the chapel and his tombstone is the second from the left on the west wall of the memorial garden.

Tombstone of the first pastor, Thomas Freeman

The inscription reflects his Calvinist theology:

Within this grave / lie deposited / the mortal remains/ of / Tho. Stev. Freeman/ who died Aug 21ˢᵗ 1821 aged 35/ Upwards of seven years / the faithful Pastor and / zealous advocate for the / cause of sovereign truth in this place / Also of Fanny Freeman / his sister / who departed this life / May 1 1821 / aged 23 / These both died in the full assurance / of faith rejoicing in their So[vereign ?] relation / in grace and unified by the blood of Jesus/ and applied by the Holy Ghost.

A series of pastors followed Thomas Freeman and the church attracted relatively large congregations. For example the 1851 religious census recorded that services were also held on a Thursday and these weekday meetings attracted a congregation of 100. The longest serving pastor was Joseph Oldfield who had completed almost 36 years of ministry when he died in 1916. His funeral was a great occasion in Godmanchester and was attended by Baptist Ministers from Brighton, Birkenhead, Plumstead, Oakham, Guildford, St Ives, Cambridge, Lakenheath, St Neots and Wellingborough. The Vicar of St Mary's Rev Cardale and Gerald Hunnybun from the Mission Hall were also amongst the mourners.[222] Joseph Oldfield was buried in the nonconformist burial ground in St Mary's Churchyard.

Great store was placed upon public baptism. Baptisms took place in the river and crowds lined the bank to witness the ceremony. One of the hymns that was sung by worshippers was, 'Ashamed of Jesus, that Dear Name?'. The practice of public baptism was later abandoned and a baptistery built in the chapel.

Particular Baptist Church Baptistery[223]

The Calvinist theology of the church is reflected in its articles of faith, 'We believe that before the world began, God did elect a certain number of the human race unto everlasting salvation'. Human frailty does not always comply with theology. The quarterly meeting books for the nineteenth century survive and provide many examples of members 'separated for bad conduct'.[224] The misdeeds of Ann Cooper, Judith Biggin, Sarah Prior and Isabella Smith were not specified. But Mr Sears' failings were that he only attended the chapel once a quarter and in 1883 he was ejected. Mr and Mrs

Wilson wrote to the Deacon to inform him that the church did not meet their standards, 'We are not able to find the least profit or edification in the ministry of Mr Oldfield'. Mr and Mrs Wilson were duly bidden farewell. A financial scandal in 1894 led to the separation of Mr Rowlatt, the church Treasurer. He refused to show the accounts for pew rents to the church and kept the money for tea and coffee sales. In the words of the deacons, this was 'conduct which would not be tolerated amongst worldly men' and Rowlatt too was separated.

There were also divisions in the church. In December 1848, a meeting was called due to the 'disturbed state of the church'. Mr Tryon was excluded from the pulpit because of his 'unchristian attacks on Mr McKenzie and other ministers of the gospel'. The supporters of Mr Tryon included leading members of the church James and Susanna Bester, Francis Tozeland and others. They too were 'separated' and some weeks later 'opened a room in Godmanchester for private worship on the Lord's Day'. Mr Tryon came to preach for this group once a fortnight.

Particular Baptist Church prior to demolition[225]

Despite these setbacks, the chapel had a large membership and a congregation more than two and a half times that of the General Baptists.

However, their fortunes changed radically in the twentieth century. By the beginning of the 1960s, the congregation had shrunk to just five people and services were held in the Manse. The Manse was Chapel House, a substantial nineteenth century house in The Stiles. In 1961, the Manse was sold and the chapel subsequently demolished. The last Pastor of the chapel was John Harwood who appears in the photograph with his wife.

John Harwood and his wife
(Reproduced by permission of Gospel Standard Library)

The memorial garden in the forecourt of the former Particular Baptist Church was redesigned and restored in 2004 under the guidance of David Comben a landscape architect and Town Councillor. David and his wife Shona were tragically killed in a car accident in 2005 and a memorial plaque to commemorate their lives has a fitting place in the memorial garden.

Memorial to David and Shona Comben

They were also remembered in the naming of Comben Drive, the road into Mansio Place, a major new housing development in the town.

Mission Hall

The former Mission Hall in St Anne's Lane was originally strictly non-denominational. The brick and slated building was built in the 1870s from funds collected by voluntary subscription. The land belonged to Martin Hunnybun in what was then known as Royal Oak Lane. In 1874, the land and building was conveyed to trustees including Bateman Brown, Martin Hunnybun and Gerald Hunnybun. The conveyance required the Trustees not to hold meetings of a denominational character in the premises. Furthermore, no meetings were to be held on the Lord's Day between 10 am. and 1 pm. or between 6 pm. and 8 pm. This was presumably to avoid any conflict with services of other churches in the town. However, this requirement does not seem to have been followed for very long. The *Hunts Post* published the times of religious services each week and the Mission Hall's services were held at 11 am. and 6.30 pm. Throughout 1916 the preacher was invariably Gerald Hunnybun, who lived in Old Court Hall.[226] Gerald Honeybun was a solicitor and clearly a man of means for he had no less than four servants recorded in the 1891 census.

Mission Hall

The non-denominational character of the Mission Hall was again emphasised when Gerald Hunnybun, registered the building as a place of worship in 1911. The congregation was defined as persons 'calling themselves Christians, not otherwise designated'. However, the Mission did not embrace all Christians for Trustees were required to be either members of the Church of England or Protestant Dissenters. In 1911, the building comprised a hall, classroom and wash house and was valued at £100. The Mission had a Sunday School. In 1916 the children had their annual summer treat. 'After a bountiful tea, they enjoyed games in Mr Hunnybun's paddock'.[227] Bert Brudenell recalls that before 'moving pictures' came to the area, John Moor used to give magic lantern shows to the children at the Mission Hall. The entrance fee to the show was one penny. 'If he put a slide upside down he was greeted with much laughter and derision' by the children. John Moor was a scrap dealer from Pinfold Lane who 'traded around the District' buying rags, bones and rabbit skins. In 1936, the Mission Hall was transferred to Trustees of the Huntingdonshire Association of Baptist and Congregational Churches. Finally in 1949 it was sold to E. W. Elphick and sons for the sum of £520 and it ceased to be a place of worship. The building is now a furniture upholstery company operated by Nick and Neil Pedlar.

Society of Friends

Society of Friends

The Society of Friends, often known as 'Quakers', was founded through a Leicestershire shoemaker, George Fox. In 1652 Fox was travelling through the north of England. He had not eaten for several days and felt 'moved by the Lord to go atop' Pendle Hill near Clitheroe. At the top of the hill, Fox 'was moved to sound the day of the Lord and the Lord let me see a-top of the hill in what places he had a great people to be gathered'. He then had a further vision of 'a great people in white raiment'. Two weeks later, Fox arrived at Sedbergh and encountered a crowd of flax workers dressed in white. Here was confirmation of his vision and Fox set out preaching that Christ was available personally and directly to the people.[228] Quakers rejected formal church services, sacraments, paid ministers and emphasised the inner voice of God. Although Cromwell tried to befriend them, their 'wild enthusiasm and disorderly conduct' antagonised the authorities.[229]

Quakerism came to Cambridgeshire in 1653 and many Quaker converts were gained at the expense of the Baptists so that there was considerable friction between the two groups. In the nineteenth century Quakers refused to pay Church Rates and in Godmanchester Quakers had their goods seized as a result.[230] Today's peace-loving Quakers are quite different from their seventeenth-century forebears. Their faith derives from the belief that each one of us can have a direct relationship with the Divine. Quakers meet in silence but a person can stand up to give 'ministry' which adherents believe represents Christ's direct teaching to the meeting. Quakers started to meet in the Rose and Crown, one of Godmanchester's many former public houses, about 40 years ago. Quakers are a relatively small religious group. In Huntingdonshire the religious census of 1851 recorded only three places of worship out of a total of 188 that were designated for Quakers. By 2005 there were only 15,775 Quakers in Britain.[231] The Society in Godmanchester is not large and has about 40 members, although attendance at worship is somewhat less than that.

Methodism

Methodism was the legacy of John Wesley. Wesley, an Anglican clergyman, underwent a conversion experience in 1738 when his heart was 'strangely warmed'. Like the General Baptists he adhered to Arminian rather than Calvinistic theology. Wesley believed that all people could be saved for Jesus had died for all and not just the elect. His mission was to reform the nation and to 'spread scriptural holiness over the land'. He regarded the whole world as his parish and organised converts into religious societies. Wesley is not without his critics. He was something of an autocrat, reflected in a nickname 'Pope John', and he had disastrous relationships with women including his own marriage.

Not all regard early Methodism as dissent. Wesley remained an Anglican to his dying day. However, Wesley's antipathy to the parish system led almost inevitably to a separation of his societies from the established church. The societies eventually joined together to form congregations and these joined to form circuits, or groups of churches. Although these churches soon split into a number of denominations, Methodists grew rapidly to become the largest nonconformist grouping in England.

Locally there is a Methodist Circuit centred in Huntingdon but a Methodist society was never established in Godmanchester. John Wesley's diary recorded his visit to Godmanchester in 1774, 'a large barn was ready, in which Mr Berridge and Mr Venn used to preach. And though the weather was still severe, it was well filled with deeply attentive people'. However, when he returned in 1788 the response was not great. Wesley wrote in his diary 'it is the day of small things here'.[232]

Salvation Army

The East London Christian Mission was formed in England in 1865 by William and Catherine Booth. William, a former Methodist minister, preached to the working classes in the streets of East London. It was a revivalist movement and its hymns were sung to music hall tunes. The organisation grew rapidly and soon changed its name to the Salvation Army. In October 1871, the Salvation Army opened the doors of its Army barracks for the first time in Godmanchester. Bird reported that the Salvation Army 'met with considerable opposition and boisterous treatment at first, especially from the rougher element' but this opposition gradually ceased.[233]

A surviving photograph taken in 1892 shows a group of fourteen members (and one child on a rug at the front of the group holding a triangle) of the Godmanchester Salvation Army Band in full uniform and with their instruments.

Early Godmanchester Salvationists 1892[234]

The violent storm which damaged the Queen Elizabeth School in 1895 also made its presence felt at the Salvation Army. A service was taking place at the time and what the *Hunts Post* described as 'a hurricane' shook the building and ripped off part of the thatched roof. The Salvation Army were not alone. Mr Pratt who lived in one of the oldest buildings in Earning Street also lost his roof and many trees were uprooted in the town.[235] In 1912, Godmanchester Salvationists needed a new building and a piece of vacant land in Pipers Lane owned by Mr W. Gadsby, became available. The new hall was erected by Mr Boydon of Deeping St James. The exterior was constructed using corrugated iron on brickwood and the interior in pine matchwood and had gas lighting.

When Godmanchester Baptist Church moved from Silver Street to East Chadley Lane, the opportunity arose for the Salvation Army to move to Silver Street. Their original meeting rooms in Pipers Lane were demolished and replaced by housing.

Former Salvation Army building, Silver Street

On 13 January 1991, Captain Sylvia Pughsley held the first meeting for The Salvation Army in Silver Street. Those taking part in the opening ceremony and the dedication of the new building included The Vicar of St Mary's, Neil Follett, Baptist Minister Andrew Whitman, Salvation Army leaders and the Bedford Congress Hall Band. However, their stay at Silver Street did not last for long and some three years ago the Salvation Army Branch in Godmanchester closed down. It is now being converted into a private dwelling known as 'Font House'.

To what extent have the changes in religious practice locally reflected those in the nation? Godmanchester cannot be considered in isolation from its immediate neighbours for Methodists and Roman Catholics worship in Huntingdon or Buckden. Even Anglicans no longer automatically worship in their parish church for many chose to travel to an Anglican Church which reflects their religious preferences. Nevertheless the religious scene in Godmanchester broadly reflects the historical interpretation that secularisation, defined by falling church attendance, began in the late nineteenth century and accelerated in the 1960s. Church attendance has continued to fall in the last quarter of a century.[236] Those that were shocked by the results of the 1851 religious census that only about half the population attended church would be aghast that now less than seven per cent do so. Furthermore, the decline in attendance is set to continue for the average age of worshippers is increasing very rapidly. In the Anglican Church the average age has risen from 37 years in 1979 to 51 years in 2009.[237] A recent study of British church attendance by birth cohort shows that those born in the 1920s and 1930s are more than twice as likely to attend church as those born in the 1970s and 1980s.[238]

Despite the decline of the Church of England, its share of total Christian worshippers has remained at about 50 per cent, no different to its share in 1851. Roman Catholics at 17 per cent of all Christians in Britain have increased their market share of Christianity but the denominations that have declined the most are the Free Churches. For example, the United Reformed Church (formerly Presbyterians and Congregationalists) has lost a staggering 43 per cent of its churchgoers since 1998. The largest Free Church, the Methodists, lost 24 per cent over the same period. In this respect, the experience of the General Baptists in Godmanchester differs from national trends. They have moved into new premises because of an expanding congregation. On the other hand, the Particular Baptists, which had a large congregation in the nineteenth century, the Salvation Army and the Mission Hall have all closed down.

Why does such a large percentage of the population call itself Christian yet not wish to attend worship in any church? No less than 4440 people, 74.1 per cent of Godmanchester's population, declared itself to be Christian in the 2001 census, just above the national figure of 71.6 per cent. Although the religion question was voluntary, no less than 92 per cent of respondents answered it in the census. Part of the reason may be the wording of the question. The British Social Attitudes Survey published in *Social Trends* in 2008 found only 50 per cent of the nation's population claiming to be Christian, a significantly lower level of commitment than in the 2001 census.[239] The census had asked 'What is your religion?' whereas the British Social Attitudes Survey question, 'Do you regard yourself as belonging to any particular religion?' may have more clearly suggested that no religion was a possible answer.[240] A further part of the explanation is that surveys always find religious profession scores much more highly than religious activity. In her book, *Religion in Britain since 1945*, Grace Davie concluded that 'More and more people within British society want to believe but do not want to involve themselves in religious practice'.[241] The phenomenon of believing but not belonging appears to be widespread and this is true in Godmanchester too.

8

EDUCATION

Elementary Education

Some form of elementary education has been provided in Godmanchester for more than six centuries. There is evidence that a chantry founded in the fourteenth century was also used for teaching purposes. During the reign of Edward VI the endowment lapsed and it passed into the hands of the king.[242] In the early modern period, village schools run by local clergymen developed somewhat piecemeal. By 1730 Huntingdonshire had 18 such schools but many villages were without a school and children faced a long walk to the nearest one or else played truant. In the nineteenth century, state funding of elementary education grew rapidly. In 1850 it was £189,000 but rose to £840,000 by 1862. Nevertheless, Britain lagged behind much of Western Europe and particularly North America in the provision of primary education.

Sunday Schools played an important supplementary role in promoting literacy prior to the 1870 Education Act. Robert Raikes, born in Gloucester in 1735, is generally regarded as the founder of the Sunday School movement. Sunday Schools spread rapidly and Godmanchester had well supported Sunday Schools. For example, on census Sunday, 30 March 1851 St Mary's Church had 289 scholars in attendance. In 1868 the Particular Baptist Church built a Sunday School for 200 children.

The purpose of education in England remained the same: to fit recipients for their proper station in life rather than to encourage people to better themselves.[243] The religious element of education was fiercely disputed. Church schools were grant aided and nonconformists objected to their taxes being used to support Anglican schools. Intense rivalry developed between Anglican National Schools and Nonconformist British Schools. Godmanchester had both a national school and a British school in Pipers Lane. Many nonconformists believed that education should be provided by voluntary action and deprived of state aid, Anglican schools would decline.

However, the cause of voluntarism was generally rejected and the National Education League campaigned for free, compulsory 'undenominational' education for every child.

William Forster's Education Act of 1870 was a response to the demands of the National Education League. The Liberals faced a dilemma for they mainly believed in voluntarism rather than compulsion. Forster's Act provided for elementary education for children aged 5-13 but parents still had to pay fees to send their children to school. Forster's Act sought to provide elementary education by means of school boards where the voluntary system was proving inadequate. In 1883 Godmanchester Town Council wrote to the Department of Education requesting the establishment of a school board for the Borough. The Vicar of St Mary's Church, Reverend Chamberlain was greatly exercised and also wrote to the Education Department requesting that the Town Council decision should be overturned. He got little change out of the Department and was informed that the Town Council decision would proceed.[244]

School attendance between the ages of five and ten was not compulsory until a subsequent Education Act in 1880. This measure was not fully effective and by 1895, only 82 per cent of children on school registers regularly attended.[245] The 1891 Education Act introduced free education and Balfour's Education Act of 1902 abolished school boards and Local Education Authorities were established under a central Board of Education. In 1918, a national minimum school leaving age of 14 was established.

The Education Act of 1944 established County Primary Schools for children up to age 11, when they sat an examination to determine the secondary school they would attend until they were 15. The most academically able went to grammar schools, the rest to secondary or secondary modern schools. The Act also created two types of successor to public elementary schools: Voluntary Aided and Voluntary Controlled schools. Voluntary Aided schools were funded by the Local Education Authority and the governing body was independent. Voluntary Controlled schools owned their buildings and the staff were employed by the governors.

Godmanchester now has two primary schools. Godmanchester County Junior School was built on the former kitchen gardens of Island Hall. The school was officially opened by the Countess of Sandwich on 6 July 1955. The new school was built for just 160 children and succeeded the former school building in St Anne's Lane. Godmanchester Community Primary School, as it later became, has had 4 Heads in its 58 year history. Miss Eileen Thakray was headmistress until 1960 when she was succeeded by Reginald Lord. Brian Brown became Head Teacher in 1983 until he was followed by Phillip Ellington in the year 2000. The first teachers at the school were Pop Hardy, Miss Hall, Mrs Dadd and Mrs Mash. An important addition to the amenities of the town was the building of the Community Pool in the school grounds. The pool was opened by the former Prime Minister John Major in 1999. About a quarter of state primary schools in England are Church of England schools. When a second primary school was built in Godmanchester it was a Church of England school: St Anne's in London Road. The first Head Teacher was Mrs Kenna and the current head is local Godmanchester man, Adrian Shepherd.

St Anne's School 1934 (Courtesy of Gerald Reeve)

Grammar Schools

Grammar Schools were established in several Huntingdonshire towns during the sixteenth and seventeenth centuries.[246] Huntingdon's Grammar School was founded in 1565, Kimbolton's in 1600 and Ramsey's in 1652.

But Godmanchester was quicker off the mark and the beginnings of the Queen Elizabeth Grammar School date back to 1558.

On 20 September 1558, Richard Robins of Godmanchester, 'being seeke of bodie but hole of mynde and parfite remembraunce' made his last will and testament. He willed that enough of his lands as necessary were to be sold to raise the rent or value of £20 per annum with which a Free Grammar School was to be endowed in Godmanchester under the supervision of a Cambridge College. He further requested that the schoolmaster was to be a priest so that every Friday and Sunday mass could be said for amongst others, his own soul, the souls of his two deceased wives, his parents and 'all christian soules'. In May 1561 at the request of the townspeople, Queen Elizabeth I issued letters-patent granting her name to the school. This is consistent with the inscription under the south porch window '*Eliz. Reg. Hujus Scholae Fundatrix*'.

Queen Elizabeth Grammar School

The Queen's charter sets out that the education and instruction in Grammar were to be taught by one master and one usher, (also known as a sub-pedagogue or hypodidascal!) and that fourteen 'honest men of Godmanchester' and the vicar of the parish were to constitute the school governors. The master lived at the west end of the building. The porch formed part of his residence and the little room over the entrance still contains a cast-iron fireplace and chimney.

Shortly after making his will Richard Robins died, little knowing what legal complications would follow. In the following year Robins' executors were brought to court and presented with a bill of complaint alleging that the lands he had left to endow the school were not legally his own. The court did not endorse the claim and the matter of endowment seemed to be resolved. However, in 1575 a long legal battle was commenced by Robins' heirs, contesting his bequest to the school. The case eventually came before the Star Chamber and a settlement was reached which resulted in the governors and Robins' heirs conveying the estate to the then Chancellor of the Exchequer, Sir Walter Mildmay. Sir Walter surrendered the estates to Emmanuel College, Cambridge for the use of the Master, Fellows and Scholars. Mildmay granted the governors of the school £20 a year from the estate to be paid from the funds of Emmanuel College, Cambridge.[247] The Grammar School's endowment of £20 per annum soon proved inadequate as a result of inflation. In 1693, the school governors agreed to elect a Treasurer whose duties were to manage the school funds in accordance with the charter of Queen Elizabeth and the wishes of the founder and to inspect the building and make a 'faithful report'.[248]

Paradoxically, 'Free' Grammar Schools often charged fees.[249] Repairs to the school were to be paid for out of scholars fees i.e. one shilling on admittance for every 'Freeborn Child' and two shillings for every 'Stranger's Child' followed by six pence every quarter. Doubtless the school was helped by such bequests as made by a Robert Stappard of Godmanchester in his will of 1639 which gave 'to the free Scoole Scollers of Godmanchester Tenn Shillings to buie them a dixanarie if it mai be recovered of Mr Evans of Cambridge'. By the early part of the nineteenth century fees for the upkeep of the building had ceased and the only income derived from the endowments went to provide a salary for the master.[250] The Friends of the Queen Elizabeth School have in their possession a 'School Pence Book' covering a period of five years from 1850 showing at that time pupils were once more asked, but did not always manage to pay a subscription of 2*d* a week for the upkeep of the school.

Grammar schools were established for teaching Latin Grammar but in Godmanchester this did not last very long. In 1704 a report of the governors' meeting stated that teaching consisted of learning to 'write and cast accounts'. A weekly timetable survives from 1831 when Mr Gaunt was the schoolmaster. Each day started with bible lessons, but the educational emphasis was on being able to read, write, spell and to have an understanding of basic arithmetic. F.W. Bird, the Borough Treasurer, gave a vivid description of Mr Gaunt whose name seemed very apt: a small stooped, slimly-built man, dressed in black with a top-hat and spectacles on his nose and often a quill pen behind his ear. He was famous for his canings, the results of which could be heard for some distance; if a boy tried to escape, Mr Gaunt would run out after him. Fox records that Mr Gaunt's salary had increased from £20 a year to £40 by an annual donation from Henry Sweeting the Borough Recorder.[251]

Forster's Education Act of 1870 had considerable consequences for the school. The grammar school only had room for 70 boys. In order to meet the Act's 'rule of sufficiency for the population of the parish', an increase in the accommodation to provide for 130 boys was required. The difference between the 70 boys attending the school and the proposed figure of 130 reflects the fact that a large number of children in the parish were not receiving formal education at this time. The governors proposed that the master should move out of the school building into a rented cottage or be provided with a house, the means for which would be obtained from the income derived from the increase in pupils. The trustees felt very strongly that this should be the way forward in funding the enlargement of the school premises as otherwise a School Board would have to be formed and 'the imposition of an education rate paid upon the Parish' which would 'create feelings of hostility and bitterness'.[252] However, the establishment of a school board was not long delayed.

Educational standards at the school were poor. Hopkins, who started teaching at the school in 1878, commented that schoolwork was in a very backward state, discipline very bad and the boys exceedingly rough. Attendance was a continual problem in an agricultural community where duties on the land took precedence. The entry for 26 June 1882 in the school log book recorded: 'miserable attendance – great number of boys away haymaking, many unqualified to go to work' and on 29 April 1884: 'a few boys are away to gather cowslips'. Concentration must also have been difficult at times. On 24 May 1882 the master reports: 'we have had a very noisy time in school today owing to the presence of two traction engines against the windows and the washing of some hundreds of sheep on the School Hill and on 19 June teaching was almost impossible due to the noise from swinging boats, toy and sweet stalls and several vans on School Hill.[253] Following Balfour's Education Act of 1902, the Queen Elizabeth Grammar School was eventually transferred to the local education authority on 7 June 1907.

A former teacher had a sharp memory of the school from 1934 until its closure after the Second World War. When interviewed at the age of 94, Stanley Batten recalled that there were three teachers and three classes of approximately thirty boys with seldom more than a hundred boys in total. The front large classroom was divided by a folding partition into two smaller classrooms. The playground was at the front of the building and is now used as a public parking area. Standards of safety have clearly changed as boys were allowed to play ball games without any railings to enclose the area, though being 'trained well not to follow the ball into the road'. On Empire Day the boys stood outside the school with flags belonging to the countries of the Empire and girls from St Anne's Girls School were allowed to join them. The school augmented its limited facilities by using spare ground Mr Batten believes was in Post Street to teach gardening, Portholme was used for nature lessons and the recreation field for swimming lessons and sports days.

Despite attempts to bring the school and its facilities up to date, the school building was becoming difficult to sustain. In June 1946 the National School Survey reported: 'General state of decay to old portion i.e. classrooms 1 & 2, cloaks & lobby. Facing bricks in decay and requires pointing. Internal walls require part plastering and decorating'. The Governors' Minute Book recorded in the same month: 'The Boys' School is in many ways unsuitable for its purpose by modern standards, and especially is unsafe on account of its position and the absence of suitable playground accommodation'. The Huntingdonshire Education Authority proposed to move boys over eleven years of age to a new secondary school in Huntingdon and those under eleven would be transferred to the existing council school for girls in Godmanchester which would then become a Junior Mixed Primary School. After almost four centuries the school vacated the premises at the end of May 1948.

Queen Elizabeth School 1944[254]

The Building and its Conservation

The Queen Elizabeth Grammar School, a Grade II listed building, now stands proudly in the heart of Godmanchester. Whilst other remaining sixteenth and early seventeenth century buildings in the town are all of timber-framed construction, the grammar school was built in red brick. Red bricks were probably used to impart a sense of status and pride in the school and to mark it out in a distinctive manner from other vernacular buildings in the town.

The repaired porch wall

In March 1895, wreckage was caused to the south side of the school by the violent storm which also caused havoc at the Salvation Army building. Apart from severe damage done to the south side of the roof, the front wall of the porch had been 'partially thrown down' bringing the sundial with it.[255] The rebuilding of this part of the building can still be clearly seen. The Royal Commission on Historic Monuments reported in 1926, that the restored sundial had a moulded cornice and the inscription 'Sibi Aliisque', perhaps referring to Richard Robins who endowed the school. Time and weather have obliterated any trace of the inscription which means 'to himself and to others'. A major extension to the building took place at the beginning of the twentieth century when a new classroom was built onto the north side of the building.[256]

When the Queen Elizabeth School closed in 1948 the governors resolved that they would 'do all in their power to secure the continued use of the school for religious and cultural purposes, to the benefit of the inhabitants of Godmanchester, in accordance with the wishes of the founder'. In 1981 a charity, the 'Friends of the Queen Elizabeth School', was founded. At that time the school was in a bad state of repair and hardly used. In 1984 a meeting called to determine ownership of the building and its future resulted in Godmanchester Town Council assuming possession of the school and taking responsibility for its renovation and adaptation for use by the town. The role of the Friends was to assist in the preservation of the school building for the benefit of the public and to preserve its character and amenities and secondly to promote recreational and leisure activities there for the benefit of local people. The restoration of the two classrooms into halls for community use also involved demolishing all the buildings in the school yard and the front wall and public toilets. New facilities were built onto the west end of the 1900 extension including a small kitchen and store cupboard and also public toilets accessible from School Hill.

The building re-opened for public use in March, 1987. The halls are hired out to a wide range of clubs and societies and also to individuals wishing to use them for private functions, generating an income to help maintain the building. Since its formation the Friends hoped that a small museum might be established in the school porch. This project was realised in 1989 and the Porch Museum opened periodically for exhibitions. Displays reflect various aspects of Godmanchester history and artefacts and photographs are contributed by people of the town.

Adult Education

Godmanchester had a Working Men's Reading Room which was established in 1859. It levied a weekly fee of one penny a week but closed down before the turn of the twentieth century. The Workers Education Association (WEA) was founded in 1903 to provide new opportunities for working people to continue learning. Godmanchester still has a thriving WEA group but its members are much more likely to be retired than in employment.

A wide range of courses ranging from science to art and history are offered to all adults whether in work, retired or unemployed. When the WEA celebrated its centenary in 2003, a party was held in Godmanchester and costumed displays were held in St Mary's Church.

Celebrating the centenary of the WEA in Godmanchester
Lynda Heseltine, Helen Hollington, Maureen Bramwell, Pam Sneath, Mary Stokes

To what extent has the investment in education been successful? One measure has been the advancement of literacy but it is not a simple concept. In the early modern period the ability to read, particularly the printed word, was much commoner than the ability to write. Furthermore there were so many different kinds of written word and such a diversity of scripts and typefaces that there was no simple contrast between literacy and illiteracy.[257] Girls were customarily taught to read the printed word but not to write. Therefore measures of female literacy based on writing ability alone would be very misleading.[258] Even book ownership did not necessarily imply an ability to read for those who owned the commonest book, a bible could not always read it. Ownership of the bible had protective qualities for the owner such as 'warding off evil spirits and keeping the devil at bay'. It was also useful for recording family births and swearing of oaths.[259] However, the percentage of adults in England that could sign their name rose rapidly during the early modern period. In 1500 only six per cent of England's adult population could sign their names, lower than many other European countries. However, by 1800 the percentage had risen to no less than 53 per cent, much higher than the rest of Europe with the single exception of the Netherlands.[260]

Education may have progressed a long way but the results of the 2001 census revealed that no less than 37 per cent of Godmanchester residents aged 16-74 had fewer than five 'O' level passes, CSE (Grade 1) or their equivalent. At the other end of the spectrum 27 per cent had a first degree or its equivalent. Nevertheless, the results for Godmanchester are better than for both the county of Huntingdonshire and England. In England 46 per cent had fewer than five 'O' level passes and 20 per cent had a first degree or its equivalent.

9

THE BUILT ENVIRONMENT

The notable buildings of Godmanchester are not confined to its churches and the Queen Elizabeth School. Godmanchester has a rich heritage of private dwellings. One of the earliest is 31 London Road which may originally date from the period 1380 to 1430.

31 London Road

It has a sixteenth-century kitchen and the dining room has a fireplace with a witch mark on the beam. A mummified toad was found there. Granville Rudd, a former owner, uncovered a treasure trove of seventeenth and eighteenth-century artefacts from the building including wine bottles, clay pipes, a chamber pot, pewter spoon, English delftware and a knife and fork. The fork is particularly interesting because whereas knives date back to the Palaeolithic period forks used for eating food are a much more recent phenomenon. In the early modern period food was often gruel or liquid and was drunk from bowls. When solid food such as bread, or meat was eaten it was cut with a knife and brought to the mouth with fingers.[261] Although relatively inexpensive it was not until the eighteenth century that forks commonly began to be owned by persons of middle rank.

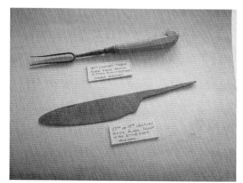

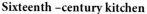

| Sixteenth –century kitchen | Knife and fork from 31 London Road |

Philip Dickenson's account of Godmanchester asserted that it was a very prosperous place, especially between the sixteenth and eighteenth centuries. For supporting evidence Dickenson pointed to the number of fine houses of freeman-yeoman type which still grace its streets. Examination of the Hearth Tax records can help to set the surviving houses in a wider context. Nearly a third of Godmanchester households had three or more hearths, which was relatively high compared with England as a whole.[262] The yeoman farmhouse, such as the few that have survived in Earning Street, would typically have had three or four hearths and those of the gentry several more. Of the largest houses in Godmanchester, that occupied by John Hearne esquire appears on both lists with nine hearths declared in 1664 and ten in 1674. On the other hand, many households were too poor to pay the tax. The Hearth Tax Act 1662 exempted from payment those already exempt from paying local taxes to the church and poor and those who 'inhabit' a house of not greater value than twenty shillings per annum. The tax returns for 1664 record that no less than 60 per cent of households (57 per cent in 1674) in Godmanchester had only one hearth or were exempt from the tax on grounds of poverty. This suggests that there were many more relatively poor houses which have not survived. The fine remaining yeoman houses in Earning Street provide a distorted picture of the community as a whole.

A survey of surviving seventeenth-century housing in Huntingdonshire was conducted by Beth Davis in 2006. She found evidence of substantial rebuilding in the early seventeenth century such as the surviving farmhouses in Earning Street, which were former hall houses. By the end of the seventeenth century the house plan had developed from the medieval hall and cross-wing into lobby-entry houses of one storey and attic or two storeys and attics.[263]

Earning Street

Earning Street has five surviving early modern houses.

Tudor House (1600-1603)

The Gables (1628)

Plantagenet House (c.1550)

A large farmhouse known as 'Tudor House' is described by Pevsner as 'the best timber-framed house in Godmanchester'. It was built in 1600-03 and restored in 1994-95 at a cost of about £1million by East Shires Trust. On the same side of the road is 'The Gables' a jettied building with the date 1628 which may be the date of rebuilding. The earliest part of the building is probably the cross-wing that is earlier than the major rebuilding. The cross-wing still has an impressive seventeenth-century fireplace.

The earlier 'Plantagenet House' was named after Edmund Plantagenet, son of Edward III, lord of the manor house that formerly stood on this site. The plaque contains the Plantagenet motto and badge 'A Dieu foy aux amis foyer' meaning 'Faith in God: a fireside for friends'. Plantagenet House was owned in the eighteenth century by John Downes a butcher and farmer. Downes paid the Sun Insurance company a premium of 16 shillings in 1761. The house and contents were insured for £200 and the barn and stable, barley barn and wheat barn for a further £200. This indicates it was once a substantial farm. A whole wing at the entrance to what is now Sylton Close was demolished when the house was restored in 1977. The upstairs back room has a seventeenth-century brick hearth and its wooden lintel still clearly shows burns from tapers.

Plantagenet House Back Room

One of the most intriguing houses in Godmanchester is Dairy Farm. The wing to the right when facing the house is early nineteenth century but the kitchen is seventeenth century. However, the back of the house is much earlier and architectural historian Beth Davis has suggested that it dates from the period 1475-1520 and that it might be a guild house.

Allen Farm

Seventeenth-century housing is not confined to Earning Street. Allen Farm is another fine example in Silver Street. This jettied building may originally date from the sixteenth century. It also has a fine fireplace and like Plantagenet House has taper burns on the timber hearth lintel which tangibly bring us into contact with the past.

Allen Farm

Island Hall

Island Hall in Post Street was built on the site of a former tannery. The red-brick building which dates from the mid-eighteenth century was built by 'Original' Jackson for his son, John. 'Original' Jackson was a merchant who was elected five times as one of the two bailiffs who governed Godman-chester. The Jacksons were joint Receivers of the Land Tax, a gift from their patron, the 4th Earl of Sandwich. In 1803 the Jacksons had to sell their in-heritance due to crippling debts and in 1804 the Baumgartner family bought the property at a public auction which took place at the Fountain Inn in Huntingdon (until 2009 the site of Woolworths). The auction notice described the house as 'an elegant double-fronted modern-built mansion of red brick' whose flower gardens communicated by a Chinese bridge with 'a delightful island of pleasure grounds' comprising 'grovage, fish ponds, walks, shrubs and fruit trees, and commanding the most perfect view of Portholme Race Ground'.

The Baumgartners originally came from Switzerland. Jacob Julian Baumgartner arrived in England in the middle of the eighteenth century and subsequently married Tryce Parrat an heiress with a considerable for-tune including land in Cambridgeshire and two farms in Godmanchester. Tryce was named after her Tryce ancestors, an old established Godman-chester family. The earliest recorded bailiff of Godmanchester was a John Tryce in 1606. One of the sixteenth century Tryces married the daughter of Richard Robins who endowed the Queen Elizabeth Grammar School. In 1816, Jacob's son Dr John Baumgartner inherited the house.

Island Hall in the nineteenth century (Courtesy Christopher Vane Percy)

Island Hall is unusual in that the front and back of the house are identical. The entrance hall is very large comprising over a third of the ground floor area with the two main reception rooms, drawing room and dining room located in the north wing. The formal area of the house is separated from the kitchen with back stairs providing access to servants' quarters.

Island Hall kitchen gardens in the 19th century (Courtesy Christopher Vane Percy)

When Dr John died in 1874, the Hall passed to General Robert Baumgartner and subsequently to Robert's daughter Violet. There were many links between the leading families of Godmanchester and hence their related properties. One example was when Violet Baumgartner married Major Frederick Beart of the Chestnuts in 1891. Sadly their marriage lasted just 4 years as Frederick died of a chill which he caught whilst skating at a Bandy Match on Bury Fen. Violet subsequently married Cyril Bevan in 1915 but this marriage was even shorter for Cyril died just a year later! Undaunted by her misfortunes Violet was to live at Island Hall for over half a century and became the last of the Baumgartner family to live there. However, by then the family name had changed to Percy which the family adopted at the time of the First World War in 1914.

The house has not remained in the continuous ownership of the Baumgartner /Percy family. Three years before Violet's death, the Hall was requisitioned by the WAAF in 1943 and in 1945 was used by the Pathfinder Squadron as an airmen's mess. At the end of the war Island Hall was taken over according to the Emergency Housing Act. By 1948 the Hall was in a very dilapidated state and the future of the building was uncertain.

Island Hall and its Chinese Bridge in 1948

The first part of the Hall to be disposed of was the former kitchen gardens which extended across to the other side of Post Street. In the early 1950s the Primary School was built on this site. Next to the kitchen gardens stood Mr Flint, the gardener's cottage which was demolished and became Unwin's Car Park. In 1958, the Hall itself was sold to the local authority and converted into flats. In 1977, a fire broke out in the south wing and the building was purchased by Simon Herrtage for just £22,000. Simon began a major programme of restoration and most of the present south wing now dates from these repairs.

When Christopher Vane Percy purchased Island Hall in 1983 it returned to the Baumgartner family, for Christopher is a seventh generation descendent from Jacob Baumgartner. In 1985 Christopher purchased the island from David Clifton and so at last the property became Island Hall in substance as well as in name. Christopher, an interior designer and former chairman of the British Interior Design Association, is an ideal person to have commenced a restoration programme for the house. Attempts have been made to restore the original designs and colour schemes and eighteenth and nineteenth century furnishings have been collected for the house.

Records associated with Island Hall reveal a fascinating first-hand account of the family's involvement in various historical events. For example the correspondence of General Robert Baumgartner (1814-1895), John and Philippa's second son, provide unique insights of his service in India and the Crimean War including the Siege of Sevastopol (1854–1855). He was also involved in the transportation of convicts to the penal colony in Australia. The records also include a collection of late nineteenth-century photographs by Alfred Hendrey which add to our understanding of the house. Octavia Hill the housing reformer and co-founder of the National Trust wrote a detailed description of the house in 1859 which can be compared with Hendrey's photographs.[264] Writing to her sister, Octavia Hill described Island Hall as 'the loveliest, dearest old house, I never was in such a one'.

Island Hall has contributed to the life of the town as the location of a number of community events. In the recent past perhaps the most notable has been May Revels which has featured maypole dancing. But at the beginning of the twentieth century Island Hall hosted Godmanchester's Water Carnival. In 1905, a water carnival was held in the grounds and more than a thousand people paid for admission. Appropriately, the profits were donated to the County Hospital with which Dr John Baumgartner had a close association. The following year the water carnival was again hailed a great success. No less than 1200 people passed through the turnstiles at Island Hall and hundreds more watched free of charge from Portholme. There was dancing on the lawn, illuminated by Chinese lanterns. The highlight of the evening was the procession of illuminated boats including a state gondola and another boat which discharged fireworks. Another attractive boat had a party of dominoes on board including a 'well known lady' who wore a mask. Mr Leete won first prize for his boat which was covered in deep red ruby lights. A Japanese Junk entered by Miss Tillard, with her crew all wearing native costume, won the second prize.[265]

The Holme

The Holme in Post Street was built in the eighteenth and nineteenth centuries. It was the home of the Tillard family who had close links with the Baumgartners. In 1834 Philip Tillard married Dr John and Philippa Baumgartner's first daughter, Julia and they lived at Island Hall for a period whist the Baumgartner's were abroad. The Tillards later took up residence at Stukeley Hall before returning to Godmanchester at the Holme.

Two years after Philip's marriage to Julia, their second son Philip Edward Tillard was born. The son Philip became a barrister and then a partner in the bank known as Vesey, Desborough and Company. The bank was subsequently incorporated into Barclay's Bank. Philip was Justice of the Peace, a Deputy Lieutenant for Huntingdonshire and was elected Mayor of Godmanchester in 1873. The Tillard family gave the large central medallion depicting the Town's emblem, the Fleur-de-Lys for the new Mayoral chain, made to commemorate Queen Victoria's Diamond Jubilee in 1897. Philip's wife, Iona was the eldest daughter of John Bonham Carter MP for Winchester and one of the great Liberal political dynasties. The Tillards had a large family and the couple produced a child almost every year in the first decade of their marriage. Confusingly their seventh child, a son was also named Philip.

A surviving photograph from 1903 shows a Tillard wedding party taken in the conservatory at the Holme. The bride is Olive Marjorie Tillard, one of Philip and Iona's daughters, who married Arthur Enfield Taylor (known as Archie). Standing next to the bridegroom is Tryce Beart, daughter of Violet Beart of Island Hall. Behind Tryce are Olive's two older sisters Edith and Laura.

Olive Tillard's marriage party 1903 (Huntingdonshire Archives)[266]

Farm Hall

Farm Hall was rebuilt in 1746 for Charles Clarke the Recorder of Huntingdon. The property has had an illustrious list of owners including Thomas Clarke, Charles' son who became Lieutenant Governor of Quebec, and Robert Towgood, Mayor of Godmanchester and founder of the Cricket club.[267] During the Second World War, Farm Hall was used as an interrogation centre by the Special Operations Executive.[268] The present owner Dr Echenique helped to uncover some of the house's secrets. Whilst carrying out renovations, Dr Echenique found extensive listening devices under the floorboards of the house.[269]

The story begins in 1938 when Otto Hahn (1879-1968) discovered nuclear fission. Hahn subsequently received the Nobel Prize in Chemistry for his work. So important was this discovery in the context of war that the AL-SOS mission was established to accompany the allied invasion of 1944 with the objective of arresting scientists working on the development of a German Atomic Bomb. Ten German scientists were seized including Heisenberg and Hahn. They landed at Tempsford on 3 July 1945 and were taken to Farm Hall by car. The scientists were held at Farm Hall for six months. Their conversations were recorded and transcripts were published in 1993. One scientist Dr Kurt Diebner correctly suspected that the Hall had been bugged but Professor Heisenberg was dismissive of such a suggestion: 'Microphones installed? Oh no, they're not as cute as all that. I don't think they know the real Gestapo methods; they're a bit old fashioned in that respect.' A fateful day was 6 August 1945 when Otto Hahn was told that the atomic bomb had been dropped on Japan. Hahn was devastated by the news and blamed himself for the scale of deaths that his discovery had made possible.

It has often been suggested that the German scientists knew how to develop a nuclear bomb, but delayed their efforts because of opposition to Hitler. In his book *Hitler's Scientists* John Cornwell rejects this view. Cornwell argued that the tapes suggest that Heisenberg and the other scientists lagged far behind in their understanding of the physics of nuclear weapons. The events at Farm Hall are also the basis of a play *Copenhagen* by Michael Frayn which was subsequently adapted as a film in 2002. The film starred no less than James Bond himself, Daniel Craig as Heisenberg, Stephen Rea as the Danish physicist Niels Bohr, and Francesca Annis as Margrethe Bohr.

The Chestnuts

The Chestnuts was the home of Frederick Beart who married Violet Baumgartner of Island Hall in 1891. Frederick Beart had made his money from the brick industry. The house passed to William Frederick Beart, who was County Magistrate in 1910. Godmanchester's annual show was held in the grounds of the Chestnuts. In 1906 there were exhibitions of fruit, flowers and vegetables with separate events for cottagers and residents. For the children there was a show of nosegays (posies) of both wild and cultivated flowers. Dancing was held on the lawns and the Kings Royal Rifles played.[270]

Fox House

Adjacent to Island Hall is a substantial Victorian house built around 1890 on the site of the house of Dr Robert Fox. The importance of Robert Fox to Godmanchester and Huntingdon life is covered in Chapter 13.

The Grove and Dial House

Three important houses in Cambridge Road are No. 3, The Grove (No. 4) and Dial House (No. 5). No. 3 dates to the mid-sixteenth century, Dial House is Georgian and dates from 1714 and The Grove is a large Victorian house built in a neo-Tudor style. Dial House has a sundial at the front of the house between the windows.

Dial House

Residents of Dial House included Miss Millicent Desborough who died in 1916 and a Council Surveyor Mr Parcell who ran Godmanchester's Boy Scouts group which met in the town on Friday evenings.[271]

Chadleigh House

Chadleigh House is a Grade II listed building with an early nineteenth century front. It was owned by the Brudenell family who still live in Godmanchester. George B. Brudenell was a local builder who was responsible for building many of the houses in Godmanchester. These included the major development in Tudor Road and the bungalows in Oakleigh Crescent. George Brudenell also had a concern for the public buildings in the town and was awarded the contract for the restoration of the Chinese Bridge. George's brother Bert Brudenell provides eyewitness accounts of Godmanchester in the early part of the twentieth century elsewhere in this book.

Chapel House

Chapel House (located at 5 The Stiles, Pinfold Lane) is an early nineteenth century building which was later extended. It is named Chapel House because it was formerly the manse of the Particular Baptist Church. In 1961 it was sold and became the home of the Thurley family. Tom Thurley was a local veterinary surgeon, and together with his wife Rachel established Anglo-Indian Concern in 1988. The mission seeks to serve the Anglo-Indian community in Chennai, South India. In 1988 Chapel House was purchased by Graham Campbell and an architectural practice, Campbell Rees Associates was established.

Hope Cottage

Hope Cottage

The history of Hope Cottage and the James family has been researched by Catherine Hadley. The house at 5 London Street was occupied by the James family who had been blacksmiths in Godmanchester as far back as the eighteenth century. The blacksmith's forge and furnace backed on to Pipers Lane. The account book of John and Alfred James covering the years 1876 to 1896 has survived and is held by Huntingdonshire Archives. The full story of the James family is the subject of a display in the Porch Museum, Godmanchester.

Inns and Public Houses

In 1830 the Duke of Wellington pioneered the Beerhouse Act which allowed any householder to get a licence to sell beer and cider for a payment of two guineas. It was a liberalising Act which allowed beer houses to open for up to 18 hours a day. Hundreds of new public houses were established following the Act and many were named after the 'Iron Duke' in gratitude. The Act also had its down side and many labourers' wages 'disappeared' into beer houses.[272] By contrast brewers often made a great deal of money and this was reflected in their rising social status during the Victorian period. Godmanchester boasted a brewery established by William Garka at the back of 21 London Street. All traces of his brewery have now disappeared.[273]

In the 1840s there were some 30 public houses in Godmanchester. Post Street had the Godmanchester Arms at the former bookshop and the Rose and Crown, now the Quaker Centre. West Street had no less than six: Uncle Tom's Cabin (no.55), The Wheatsheaf (Rose Cottage), Rickyard (no.7), The Vine, The Lord Nelson (no.21) and The Shepherd and Dog (no.31). The Shepherd and Dog has the date 1593 in the south-west gable. In London Street there were five including the Musicians Arms (no.34) and the Plough (no.26). By 1915 the number of licensed houses had reduced to 12. The Chief Constable's report for that year stated that 13 persons in Godmanchester had been convicted for drunkenness. Ten were 'natives' and 3 were 'strangers'.[274]

Riverside Mill

Riverside Mill was built between 1853 and 1861 by Charles Veasey for oil cattle cake manufacturing.[275] Power for the mill was supplied not by water but by a large coal-fired steam engine. The process involved crushing and heating linseed to express the oil and pressing the residue into cattle cake. The entrance to the unloading dock to accommodate barges bringing in the linseed can still be seen.

Bird reported that the employees were men and boys from Godman-chester, supplemented by a party of men from Yorkshire. This is supported by the 1861 census which recorded that six of the ten oil millers came from Yorkshire. Many of the oil millers lived in Adelaide Terrace built by Veasey to house his employees. In 1924 Klinger Stern converted the building into a hosiery mill. A careful examination of the side of the building reveals the name Klinger Stern is still just visible. During the Second World War over 300 people were employed in the mill producing underwear, socks and sweaters for the British and United States Forces and utility garments for the domestic market.[276] The mill closed in 1972 and ten years later H. C. Moss (Builders) purchased the building and converted it into 92 residential flats.[277]

The Town Hall

The Town Hall was built in Jacobean style by Abbott and Habershon in 1844. It was enlarged in 1899 whilst W. Gadsby J.P., was Mayor and re-stored in 1979 and 1987 by the Town Council.

The Town Hall

The Town Council Office opened in the old Town Hall on School Hill on 4 January 1999. It now provides an office for the Town Clerk and the Senior Citizen's Club also meets in the building.

Two Chinese Bridges

The Chinese Bridge between the Town Hall and the Queen Elizabeth School is very precious to the people of Godmanchester because it is one of the most important images of the town.

The Town Chinese Bridge

However, there is not just one Chinese Bridge but two. The second Chinese bridge connects Island Hall to its island and was built in the eighteenth century, much earlier than the town bridge. In 1928 a violent storm caused an elm on the island to crash down on to the bridge resulting in serious damage. Although repairs were made, the bridge was not properly maintained and it was finally demolished in 1972. The current bridge is a replica erected in 1988. Christopher Vane Percy won several awards for the bridge including a Conservation Award from Huntingdonshire District Council and the Cambridge Association of Architects Craftsmanship Award.

Chinese Bridge Island Hall

Why are there two Chinese Bridges in Godmanchester? In the eighteenth century there was a great fashion for what became known as Chinoiserie. The word comes from the French for Chinese, 'chinois' and was a style inspired by art and design from not just China, but Japan and other Asian countries. It influenced paintings, prints, tapestries, costumes, textiles, illustrated books, porcelain, and furniture. Even pagodas were built in gardens and a well known example is the Pagoda at Kew Gardens, London. Godmanchester followed this love for all things Chinese and so the two bridges were built.

The town bridge was built in 1827 to relieve congestion in Mill Yard. Mill Yard was leased to Mr Ashley who contributed £100 towards the erection of the original town bridge. The decision to build a Chinese bridge was taken at a meeting of the Town Bailiffs and assistants but the vote was close and was carried by a majority of just one. When our iconic town bridge was taken down and replaced by a new one in 2010 it might have been upsetting for some residents.

The new bridge 2010 (reproduced by permission of Alan Hooker)

However, neither of the two Chinese Bridges in Godmanchester is original and they have been replaced or repaired several times. For example, in March 1959 the Borough Council was informed that the town bridge was beyond repair and was closed. The replacement bridge was built by George Brudenell at a cost of just £1,580. At its opening in 1961 the Mayor of Godmanchester declared his satisfaction with the project, 'I think it will be agreed that this new bridge is both substantial and graceful and is a credit to the local craftsmen employed in its construction'.

The architect of the original town bridge, James Gallier has an interesting story. Gallier was born in Ravensdale, County Louth, Ireland in 1798. The Godmanchester Bridge was one of his early commissions as a relatively young man in 1827. As well as designing Godmanchester's Town Bridge, Gallier was employed as Clerk of Works to the new Huntingdon Gaol. Ironically in 1828, Gallier and the mayor became involved in a fierce dispute. Gallier had been buying materials from the mayor but found that he could buy them more cheaply elsewhere. The mayor retaliated by banning Gallier from crossing his land but not to be outdone Gallier forced the gate and there was a skirmish. As a result Gallier was sent to Marshalsea prison in London![278] Gallier also worked on the redevelopment of the Grosvenor Estate in Mayfair but went bankrupt, and emigrated to America in 1832.

In America Gallier made his name as a notable architect. In New Orleans he established a successful partnership with Charles one of the Dakin brothers. They designed several important buildings in the Greek Revival style but the partnership lasted for only one year. Gallier had a rocky relationship with the Dakin brothers and was often in court testifying against them about the new buildings going up in New Orleans. James Gallier continued alone and several of his buildings are now National Historic Landmarks. His most important design was New Orleans City Hall in Lafayette Square. It is considered the most notable surviving example of Greek revival architecture in New Orleans.

Gallier was no stranger to personal tragedy in his life. His first wife Elizabeth died in her mid-forties but she had already given birth to their son James Gallier, Junior who also became an architect. Gallier married again to Catherine who was 24 years his junior. Several years later in 1868 they were travelling from New York to New Orleans on the paddle-steamer Evening Star but it sank in a hurricane, just off Cape Hatteras in Carolina. Both Gallier and Catherine were drowned.

Between Gallier's Chinese Bridge and Mill Yard car park, Queen's Walk is one of the most picturesque parts of Godmanchester. The trees along the bank were planted to commemorate the coronation of Queen Elizabeth II.

The Queen's Walk

Two Vanished Buildings

The Old Mill

At the end of Queens Walk the former Old Mill stood adjacent to the Mill Sluice and Mill Yard car park. This three-gabled weather-boarded building was the last surviving water mill in Godmanchester and by the 1920s it had been derelict for a considerable time. The doors and windows of the mill had disappeared and the woodwork was rotten leaving gaping holes through which the wind howled. Finally, on 4 May 1927 Kenneth Hunny-bun the Town Clerk invited tenders for the demolition of the Old Mill. Very few traces of the mill remain.

The Old Mill (Norris Museum)

Potto Brown's Flour Mill

Potto Brown (1797–1871) was born in Houghton where his bronze bust proudly stands in the square. As a boy he attended Huntingdon Grammar School (now Hinchingbrooke School) and followed in his father's footsteps to become a miller. His father ran the picturesque mill at Houghton now administered by the National Trust. When he took over from his father, Potto Brown and his partner Joseph Goodman built up a thriving milling business. Brown's business philosophy was always to use the best milling machinery and the new Godmanchester mill built in 1861 had the latest roller machinery. The building stood eight storeys high and was located next to the railway line so providing the most efficient distribution links for the flour. The building was demolished in 1969.

Mr Brown's Steam Flour Mill (Huntingdonshire Archives)[279]

10

POVERTY, CRIME AND HEALTH

Attempts to both control and provide for the poor and destitute has a long and complex history. The *Statute of Cambridge* (1388) often regarded as the first English poor law, introduced regulations restricting the movements of labourers and beggars. Each county 'hundred' became responsible for relieving those who were incapable of work because of age or infirmity. Servants wishing to move out of their own hundred needed a letter of authority from the 'good man of the Hundred' — the local Justice of the Peace — or risked being put in the stocks. Following the Dissolution of the Monasteries (1536-39) responsibility of the impotent poor passed to the parishes. The new arrangements, which evolved over a long period, were funded from the poor rate and administered by Overseers of the Poor. The able-bodied poor were given work and the impotent poor (orphans, widows, the sick and elderly) were given either 'indoor relief' in almshouses or poorhouses or 'outdoor relief' in the form of cash payments.

The Poor House

The Godmanchester Poor House was in Pinfold Lane, which also became known as 'Workhouse Lane'. Susan Oosthuizen has attempted to reconstruct the building from the record of the house's contents drawn up in 1797.[280] Her reconstruction suggests a parlour, kitchen and spinning room on the ground floor with three chambers above. A later extension provided an additional room on the ground floor, an extra chamber above and a garret room on the second floor. The contents suggest overcrowding for there were no less than 32 beds in the building including 8 beds in the chamber over the spinning room. The spinning room reveals the type of work that the resident poor were required to do.

The Master of the Poor House was William Reeve, 'a man of large physique, always well dressed in black clothes and tall hat'. William Reeve was a man of strong opinions and his particular hobby horse was the new railways 'that will be the ruination of the country'. Reeve died in 1847 aged 79. The Poor House was subsequently converted into a lodging house and finally demolished.[281]

Accounts detailing outdoor relief paid by the Overseers of the Poor also survive. They bring to life details of the people of Godmanchester who otherwise would be lost to us. The accounts set out pensions paid to widows and clothing supplied to the poor. In the three years 1787-89, there were payments for shoes, stockings, breeches, coats, waistcoats, shirts, shifts, hats, a gown, a petticoat, an apron and a handkerchief. In each case the price of the item is recorded. By far the most common item of clothing supplied was a pair of shoes. Men's shoes typically cost three shillings and six pence a pair. A number of men and boys were supplied with a coat, waistcoat and hat varying in price from eight shillings to twelve shillings. Breeches ranged from three shillings to seven shillings a pair. There are glimpses of the sick and dying. In 1787, Mary Cox was paid one shilling and six pence for nursing Ann Grange for 10 days and a further three shillings for lodging the Grange family for three weeks. Widow Jacques senior and Widow Jacques junior received three shillings for laying out John Hide and John Boswatch received nine shillings for making the coffin. Both the Jacques widows sat up all night to safeguard John Hide's body and to ensure that there was somebody present if the corpse revived. This custom of sitting up all night watching the body applied to both rich and poor.

Charitable payments supplemented those made by the Overseers of the Poor. Charity did not stop with the dissolution of the monasteries for Protestants also believed in charity. But charitable gifts no longer yielded years off of purgatory because it had been abolished. Bequests in wills became more secularised and chantries to say masses for the dead gave way to almshouses for the elderly, schools and fuel and clothing for poor. In Godmanchester, various charities for the poor were established. For example, in 1578 Robert Grainger gave and appointed as much bread as could be made of a coomb of wheat, to be made into halfpenny loaves, and distributed among the poor of Godmanchester by the churchwardens, to be charged on his mansion house in Godmanchester. Funds for two almshouses in Pinfold Lane were provided by Mrs Barbary Mansor in 1738.

These almshouses were rebuilt in 1859. Other Godmanchester charities included Sweetings Charity, Banks' charity fund for the relief of the poor and the Helen Ashton Charity.

The Poor Law amendment Act of 1834 finally abolished the old system and introduced poor law unions run by boards of elected guardians. Many parishes joined together into a union of parishes and built a workhouse. The parish of Godmanchester became part of the Huntingdon Union and a new workhouse was built in 1837 on the corner of St Peter's Road and Ermine Street in Huntingdon.

Illegitimate children were also provided for out of Poor Rate funds. Before the Poor Law Amendment Act of 1834, Overseers of the Poor tried to establish the identity of the father of an illegitimate child. The object was to require the father to pay regular amounts to the mother for the child's upkeep. Bastardy examination records for Godmanchester reveal the names of several alleged fathers who lived either in Godmanchester or further afield. An amusing example was the examination of Ann Mayes on 25 July 1811who claimed that Septimus Thong, Veterinary Surgeon of Huntingdon, was the father of her unborn child.[282]

Crime

In the medieval period, groups of ten households were accountable to the manor court for the good conduct of their households. Each household group elected a tithingman who was responsible for presenting miscreants to the manor court. The post of tithingman subsequently became the Parish Constable. The parish constable was responsible for the stocks, the pillory, whipping vagrants and escorting prisoners to the quarter sessions.

Penalties for crime were harsh by modern standards. The philosophy of punishment was deterrence. You were hanged not for stealing a horse but to stop horses from being stolen. Sheep stealing was made a capital offence in 1741. One of the few remaining gibbets in England can be seen just outside Godmanchester at the Caxton crossroads on the A1198. Three men hung for stealing sheep were buried at the site.

The death sentence was frequently not carried out and pardons were common. Almost half of those condemned to death in the 1730s and 1740s received a royal pardon. An alternative was transportation to the colonies. Some 50,000 convicts were transported to America and the West Indies between the passing of the Transportation Act in 1718 and 1775.[283] Australia was subsequently founded as a penal colony in 1788. The Huntingdonshire records show that stealing a sheep could result in 14 years transportation. Putting someone in prison for theft was expensive and so whipping or a month of hard labour was considered a better option.

At Courts of Quarter Sessions Justices of the Peace tried criminal cases and referred capital offences and other serious crimes to the next Assize Court. They met at least four times each year giving rise to their title 'Quarter Sessions'. Huntingdonshire Quarter Sessions records reveal that common crimes were theft and assault. The social historian Roy Porter wrote that 'violence was as English as Plum pudding' and three sample cases from the records show that this was true for Godmanchester.[284] In 1827 Fryce Martin of Godmanchester was prosecuted for assaulting, with intent to murder, Richard Church. The prompt action of Robert Matson, farmer, prevented the murder taking place. In 1828, Daniel Egan, a Godmanchester Shoemaker, was assaulted by William Deighton and James Mehew who had thrown Egan into the river as he was walking on Godmanchester Common. In 1828 a deposition from William Thackray of Godmanchester accused Thomas Matson, Godmanchester, of assault. This was probably the William Thackray who got Mary Weems pregnant when she was 14.

Godmanchester had its own 'lock up' with two cells on School Hill. This was used to hold people overnight and those that were 'drunk and disorderly' were put in the lock up until they sobered up. A 'lock up' which still survives can still be seen locally at Broughton, just off the A141 road near Old Hurst.

Following the Rural Constabulary Act of 1839 towns and counties in England were allowed to set up their own police forces. One of the few local towns that responded was Godmanchester. The County and Borough Police Act 1856 required police forces to be established and Huntingdon County constabulary was set up in as a result. In 1965 Huntingdonshire constabulary merged with several other police forces to create the Mid-

Anglia constabulary and in 1974 this became Cambridgeshire Constabulary with their headquarters based at Hinchingbrooke Park.

The nature of crime has changed dramatically since the medieval period when murder represented nearly a fifth of all recorded crime. Crime statistics are not always easy to interpret. However, in the year 2000 there were almost 3,500 recorded thefts and 1,600 burglaries for every murder in England. We are fortunate that in Godmanchester crime rates are considerably less than the national average.

Sickness and Health

Godmanchester has not always been a healthy place to live. It not only experienced the plague but typhoid, typhus and tuberculosis were also common. A main drainage system was provided in 1853 but sewage was deposited in the river albeit a mile and a half from the town. In 1906 there were still 192 deaths per 1,000 infants aged under one year.

Health services for the residents of Godmanchester were first organised in Huntingdon. General medical practice was established by Dr Jonah Wilson in the Market Square Huntingdon in 1821. A branch surgery was opened in Godmanchester.

Roman Gate Surgery

The Godmanchester practice was established in Old Court Hall in 1982 and transferred to the new Roman Gate Surgery in 1994. The new surgery was built on the site of the Roman Gate Garage operated by Jack Trigwell. It is named Roman Gate for it is very close to the site of the town's West Gate in the Roman period.

Huntingdonshire Infirmary and Dispensary was funded by public subscription and opened in 1789. Further public subscriptions led to the building of the Town and County Hospital in Huntingdon in 1853. There were further extensions to the building during the nineteenth century but services were transferred to the new Hinchingbrooke Hospital in 1983. Contemporary demands upon health services always outstrip the ability to provide funding for them and Hinchingbrooke Hospital in particular ran up large accumulated debts. Governments of all shades have often sought to resolve the conundrum through administrative change. There have been numerous reorganisations of health services since the National Health Service came into being in 1948. At the time of writing, further administrative change is in prospect as Hinchingbrooke Health Care NHS Trust seeks a new partner to run the hospital under an operating franchise.

Wood Green Animal Shelter

In the twentieth century, animal welfare developed to match that provided to humans and Godmanchester became an important centre of these activities in the 1980s. In 1984 Wood Green Animal Shelters purchased 52 acres of farmland and the Godmanchester shelter was opened in 1987 by H.R.H. the Princess Royal. The charity's headquarters are now based in Godmanchester. The shelter provides a temporary home to a variety of animals including dogs, cats, small animals and field animals. It also aims to 'provide help, support and guidance' for pet owners.

The charity was founded by Louisa Snow in 1924 and started its work in a small house in North London. It sought to alleviate the problem of abandoned and injured animals in London after the First World War. When Dr Margaret Young became involved with the charity in 1933 it changed its aims to finding new homes for these animals. A Hertfordshire pig farm was purchased in 1954 to take on the increasing numbers of dogs and cats being brought in and provided the charity with improved facilities to house the animals. The charity now takes in over 5000 animals a year and attracts over 400,000 visitors. In 2009 the charity employed over 200 people and had over 250 volunteers.

11

WAR AND CONFLICT

Conflicts and war have had a considerable impact on the history of God-manchester. Godmanchester owes its existence to a military establishment: a Roman fort. Its road system was laid out following the re-conquest of the town by Edward the Elder. The need to raise money for war with the French was one of the reasons for the granting of charters including that for Godmanchester in 1212. The bridge between Huntingdon and God-manchester was the scene of a significant stand by supporters of King Richard II during the Peasants' Revolt. The Peasants' Revolt was the violent response to the introduction of a Poll Tax. As rioting and killing spread out from London in the summer of 1381, the 'rebels' had to cross the stone bridge on their way to Lincoln. They had met little initial resistance and had burned down the Savoy Palace of John of Gaunt in the Strand, beheaded the Archbishop of Canterbury and forced King Richard II to cower in the Tower of London. But the people of Huntingdon, led by William Wightman, stood firm on the bridge and resisted the advance. A couple of 'rebels' were killed and the remainder ran away. So the bridge at Godmanchester proved more successful in resisting the rioting peasants than the great London Bridge had done a few days earlier. The delighted King Richard II formally thanked the town of Huntingdon for its loyalty and awarded Wightman a generous pension.[285]

Godmanchester did not escape the impact of the Civil War in the seventeenth century. In August 1645 after his defeat at the Battle of Naseby King Charles I entered Huntingdon. The king was welcomed and the Mayor of Huntingdon and two of Godmanchester's bailiffs imposed a tax on the two towns in order to present the proceeds to the king. Whilst King Charles stayed at the George in Huntingdon many of his soldiers were billeted at The Angel in Godmanchester. Other soldiers stayed at houses in the town and their occupants were obliged to provided food and drink for both men and horses.[286] The financial burdens on the local population were crippling and in Godmanchester John Robince could not raise the enormous sum of £300 demanded of him. As a result he was tortured by the Royalists. Lighted matches were placed between his fingers and he was tied up and left in his barn for the night. Many other townspeople were robbed of their money, goods and horses.[287] Fortunately for Godmanchester Charles I stayed for only two days and set off for St Neots and Bedford.

Captain James Molineux RN served under Lord Nelson during the Battle of the Nile on August 1-2 1798. The British fleet led by Horatio Nelson destroyed a French fleet anchored near Alexandria, leaving Napoleon's army in Egypt stranded. In Pigot's Directory, Captain Molineux is listed as living in Post Street in 1830. He died in 1833 and is buried in St Mary's churchyard next to the tomb of Dr John Baumgartner. His tombstone is now difficult to read but it states:

> *Sacred to the memory of Captain James Molineux RN*
> *who died September 8th 1833 aged 74 years*
>
> *He was an officer of acknowledged merit and fought under Nelson*
> *at the Battle of the Nile. His life had been long actively and lived*
> *in the service of his country.*

General Robert Baumgartner of Island Hall fought in the Crimean War. His eyewitness accounts are preserved in correspondence on display in Island Hall. Robert's letter of 10 September 1855 was written from the camp before Sevastopol and the following brief extract records the final fall of town following an eleven month siege:

> *Long, long before this reaches you my own dearest Mother, you will*
> *have heard the important news, that the impregnable Sebastapol has at*
> *last fallen, and that the Malakoff, the Redan and all the Forts on the*
> *South side, are with the Town itself in our possession. I rode down to*
> *the unhappy place yesterday afternoon, and such a scene of desolation*
> *as I witnessed, it is almost impossible to describe- The town was every-*
> *where in flames: the streets were strewn with furniture of every descrip-*
> *tion, mixed up with fragments of shell and round Shot. I did not per-*
> *ceive a single house entire*

The memorial to Huntingdonshire men who died in the Boer War (1899-1902) stands on the corner of George Street and High Street, Huntingdon, adjacent to All Saints Church. It contains the name of James John Sandifer from Godmanchester who died of disease on 23rd June 1900 at Noupoort, South Africa where he is buried. An Anglican church built by British troops stationed at Noupoort during the Boer War commemorates their fallen comrades.

The stone War Memorial on the green in front of The Black Bull was unveiled on 1st January 1921 by Major-General Pilcher. It was funded by public subscription and contains the names of 77 men of Godmanchester who died in World War I. The memorial was re-dedicated in 1947 when 13 further names for World War II were added.[288]

Godmanchester War Memorial

One of the 77 who died in World War I was Private George Leonard Page. George joined up in September 1914 and served in the First Battalion of the Bedfordshire Regiment. He was the son of George Robert and Annie Page, of Weston House, Cambridge Road, Godmanchester. A letter written to his parents in July 1915 has been preserved:[289]

Dear Mother and Father,

We are still at rest and I am writing this in a big barn in a farmyard. The barn is our sleeping and dining apartment. There are about fifty fellows here altogether. We are as happy as sand boys. Three generals have been to inspect us and one said how proud he was of the Bedfords;

for there was not a regiment in the British Army that had done more good.

When we go in the trenches again we are going to another part of the country, instead of to our old position. We have all tinned stuff like bully beef in the trenches. We get plenty of bacon which we cook ourselves so I am getting quite an expert at cooking.

Much love

G

Less than three weeks before the armistice with Germany was signed in a railroad carriage at Compiègne, France, George died from his wounds on Thursday 24th October 1918. He was just 22 years old.

Another who died was Mr and Mrs Bester's eldest son. In 1916 they received the news that Private Bester had been killed on September 30th about 12 noon:

'We were in a trench line some little distance from the front line trenches when a Bosche shell burst over our trench. Private Bester was killed instantly and knew no pain. He was buried some distance from the spot and among other comrades'.[290]

A service held in St Mary's Church, Godmanchester in August 1916 on the second anniversary of the beginning of the war left little doubt that God was on the British side. Rev Cardale preached on Psalm 124 and pointed out how much we had to thank God for during the whole of the campaign. The service closed with the hymn 'Fight the Good Fight' and 'God save the Queen'.[291] A civic service still takes place each year at the War Memorial to remember those who lost their lives in the service of their country. The sentiments of today's services are somewhat less stridently patriotic as those in the height of battle.

The Huntingdonshire Cyclist Battalions were formed just before the onset of the First World War. The Honorary Colonel in Chief was the Earl of

Sandwich and Colonel Roland Herbert the commanding officer. Colonel Herbert was appointed to his post on 27 February 1914. Extensive research on the battalion has been carried out by Martyn Smith and full details can be found on the web site: http://www.huntscycles.co.uk. The web site identifies Frederick Dighton, the son of Mr and Mrs T. Dighton, New Street, Godmanchester, who was posted to France on 26 July 1916 as part of the battalion. In 1917, Frederick Dighton was hospitalised as a result of gunshot wounds through his left arm and in 1918 he was awarded the military medal.

The Second World War impacted on the life of Godmanchester in varied ways. Most poignantly Godmanchester lost a further 13 men whose names are recorded on its war memorial. Secondly the threat to life and limb was brought to the home front. The presence of so many airfields in Huntingdonshire meant that the threat of air attack was real. Alconbury, Wyton and Gransden airfields were all attacked by the Luftwaffe. Incendiaries were dropped on Godmanchester itself but the damage was relatively minor. A farm and a house were damaged and cabbages destroyed on allotments.[292] Protecting the general public from air attack was a challenge as providing air raid shelters was expensive. Many places in Huntingdonshire including Ramsey, St Ives and St Neots had none. However, two small shelters were provided in Godmanchester: at the Holme in Post Street and in West Street.[293]

A third impact on the town was the arrival of evacuees from London. In the 1930s the government debated a policy of evacuating vulnerable groups of civilians to reduce the chaos expected to result from air attacks on cities. By May 1938 the London County Council approved the principle of evacuating all its schoolchildren. This was put into effect at the beginning of September 1939 immediately prior to the outbreak of war when over 600,000 London schoolchildren were evacuated. Several thousand of those children came to Huntingdonshire. In Godmanchester, children were accommodated at The Holme, Riverlea and the Grove.[294]

Evacuation could be very traumatic for a young child. Margaret Faulkner relates her experience of being evacuated from Hornsey at the tender age of four, 'I was to be evacuated to the country for war was imminent and parents had been persuaded to send their children to safer areas'. Arriving in Needingworth she was extremely unhappy with the family 'who just didn't seem to like me very much'. Happily she was reunited with her mother who had also been evacuated to Godmanchester. Now she lived with the Garrard family at Riverside 'a big house opposite the War Memorial'.[295]

By 1940 evacuation was becoming a major problem. In October the *Hunts Post* reported that Huntingdonshire now has 'well over 10,000 refugees (evacuees)' but more than half were unofficial evacuees. The Chief Billeting Officer for Huntingdon Borough complained that it was 'now practically impossible to find accommodation for any more mothers and children'. The penalty for refusing a billet could be as much as a £50 fine or three months imprisonment. Nevertheless there were those who objected to accommodating evacuees. A Godmanchester man Ernest Fairy was summoned to the police for failing to comply with a billeting notice. He protested that he was happy to have a child but not 'strange women' on his premises![296]

Observing the blackout caused problems for some residents. John Parker of the Railway Tavern was fined £1 for having a light showing from the back of the property. Florence Holmes of Old Court Hall was fined five shillings for riding her bicycle at 10.45 pm. and not complying with lighting restrictions because her front lamp was too bright. On the other hand Herbert Danson was fined the much greater sum of twelve shillings and six pence for having no lights on his bicycle.[297] More disturbing to the community was hooliganism caused by drunkenness. The Chief Constable expressed his concern about the number of people on the streets when night bombing was taking place. The Quarter Sessions reported that servicemen were major offenders as they got 'hopelessly drunk' and after public houses closed, they caused mayhem on the streets.[298]

Despite these minor misdemeanours the people of Godmanchester did their best to support the war effort. Parcels were sent to Godmanchester boys fighting overseas. A target of 140 parcels was set for 1940 and various fund raising events were held including dances in the Church Hall. Much more ambitious was the Spitfire Fund. Godmanchester raised £453 out of

£4,459 raised in Huntingdonshire. Lord Sandwich proudly sent off the cheque to Lord Beaverbrook in December 1940.[299]

The end of the Second World War was a cause of great celebration. Huntingdon was 'ablaze with flags' on Victory in Europe Day and the mayor gave a speech in the market square. Two returned POWs waited on the children at a street party in Cowper Road. Godmanchester also had a great display of flags and an effigy of Hitler was on show. The mayor Alderman Pettit and the Corporation attended a service at St Mary's Church which now could be floodlit. Japan was still to be defeated but Winston Churchill declared that 'We may allow ourselves a brief period of rejoicing'. Godmanchester agreed and the end of Winston Churchill's speech was greeted with a peal of bells.[300]

12

LEISURE

Rising wages after the Black Death in the fourteenth century meant that more money was available for enjoying leisure time. Drink and gambling attracted much of the surplus cash. Many workers preferred greater leisure time to earning more money once basic needs were satisfied. The feast of 'St Monday' whereby workers took Monday off every week was celebrated by many. It was argued by moralists that high wages bred laziness, disorderliness and debauchery. These 'injurious practices' included tea-drinking which was considered a waste of time and destructive of industry. Such views were widely held by contemporaries. The influential Dutch historian Jan De Vries has argued against lack of ambition by working people and for an 'industrious revolution' beginning in the mid-seventeenth century. This involved a reduction in leisure time and greater earnings allowing the household to buy more goods.[301]

The industrial revolution led to a substantial increase in the number of hours worked by the nineteenth century. Action was taken later in the century to introduce statutory bank holidays so that at least certain days could be celebrated as communal holidays. The Bank Holiday Act passed in 1871 designated four Bank Holidays: Easter Monday, Whit Monday, the first Monday in August and Boxing Day. Christmas Day, Good Friday and Sundays were already commonly recognised as holidays and not included in the Act. At the turn of the twentieth century most workers had Saturday afternoon off but paid holidays were not a statutory requirement until 1938.[302] The number of hours worked per week and holiday entitlements vary between occupations and between the sexes. People in the United Kingdom currently work an average of 1,530 hours per year, among the longest hours in the European Union but considerably less than in the United States.[303] Whatever amount of leisure time Godmanchester people have there are many facilities available.

The Comrades Club

One organisation that has provided leisure facilities to the town for most of the twentieth century is the Comrades Club. The club in Cambridge Street was formed immediately after the First World War for the comrades who had fought in that war. It now provides a wide range of leisure facilities including Super League darts, pool and snooker. There are Saturday night dances and line dancing on Wednesdays. It serves beer, wines and spirits and plays host to music and other entertainment events.

The Community Association

The prospect of a local celebration for the Queen's Silver Jubilee in 1977 triggered the birth of the Community Association. A constitution for the Community Association was adopted 'to promote and facilitate social and leisure activities for the mutual benefit and wellbeing of the community of the residents of the borough of Godmanchester'. The major event organised by the Community Association is the successor to 'Feast week' now known as Gala Week. It takes place at the beginning of July and begins with the traditional open bowls competition at the Royal Oak Bowls Club. During the week activities such as a disco, quiz night, boules and a fun run take place at various locations in the town. The climax is the final weekend. Gala day is held on the Recreation Ground and the week concludes with Picnic in the Park on the Sunday. Worship in the park organised by local churches is followed by the annual Duck Race at noon. A number of bands perform various styles of music during the afternoon. A second event arranged by the Community Association is the ever popular firework display on November 5th at Judith's Field.

Godmanchester in Bloom

A household survey in England found that gardening was the favourite leisure activity of more than half of those questioned.[304] The people of Godmanchester do not appear to disagree. Residents spend a great deal of time in their gardens and the judges of the recently established Godmanchester in Bloom have many possible candidates for their garden competitions.

Godmanchester in Bloom was established with the aim of bringing people together to enhance the environment through floral displays, permanent planting and other measures. In its short life it has already extended the number of hanging baskets, planted trees and sowed a wild flower meadow. The osier beds near the lock are also being restored. The plan is to use the old osier trees and cuttings taken from them to create a habitat that will attract wildlife. Winners of a front garden competition have included 23 East Chadley Lane and Ed Goddard from New Street. In 2008, Godmanchester entered the Anglia in Bloom competition and gained a Silver Award in the Small Town category and won the Environmental Quality Award category.

Godmanchester in Bloom 2010

In 2010 Godmanchester in Bloom introduced two further innovations: an open gardens day and a scarecrow festival. The sight of female scarecrows hanging from upstairs windows in streets in the town produced some initial alarmed responses until passers-by realised what they were seeing was not humans about to jump!

Scarecrow at the Vicarage

Scarecrows in Earning Street and Old Court Hall

Allotments

Flowers and vegetables are cultivated on the allotments at Cambridge Road. Godmanchester and District Allotment Association is part of a national organisation, the National Society of Allotment and Leisure Gardeners. The history of allotments can be traced back to the availability of common land prior to enclosure. The General Enclosure Acts of 1836 and 1840 enabled landowners to enclose land without recourse to parliament but the General Enclosure Act of 1845 provided for land to be set aside for allotment use. This 1845 act established the present system of allotments by requiring Commissioners to make 'field gardens' limited to a quarter of an acre available to the landless poor.

During both the First and Second World Wars food shortages increased demand for allotments. The 'Dig for Victory' campaign encouraged the public to produce their own food and even public parks were used for food production. Following a peak of 1,400,000 in 1943 there was a sharp decline in allotment provision to around 500,000 by the 1970s. The decline continued and by 1996 less than 300,000 plots were available. More recently allotments have increased in popularity as a result of rising food prices, concerns about genetic modification of food, pollution and the attraction of fresh food. There are now waiting lists for sites that previously had high vacancy rates.

Cinemas

The popularity of film meant that the number of cinemas grew rapidly in the twentieth century. As early as 1914 there were 3,000 cinemas in Britain and at the outbreak of the Second World War there were 5,000. No less than twenty million cinema tickets were sold each week.[305] The introduction of speech in 1927 and subsequently colour greatly increased the attraction of films. Godmanchester people attended local cinemas in Huntingdon. The Grand and The Gem both opened before the beginning of the First World War. The Grand was built on the site of what is now the 99p stores and it could seat about 500 people. In 1916 the Grand was advertising Charlie Chaplin in the film 'Nothing but trouble' during the height of the fighting. Ironically four weeks earlier the film being screened was 'Thou *shalt not kill'* featuring Blanche Sweet![306] The Gem did not last long and closed in 1922 but was later replaced by the Hippodrome in 1934. After the Second World War cinema attendances reached an all-time high. Cinema goers in Huntingdon were not so lucky. The Grand burned down in 1954 and in 1971 the Hippodrome decided to host Bingo instead of films. By the time that Huntingdon once again had a cinema, the Cromwell in 1984, the boom times were over. Customers who had not been beguiled by television now preferred more choice. The new out-of-town Cineworld which opened in the millennium year with its multi screens provided it. Such fierce competition led to the rapid demise of the Cromwell.[307]

Sport

Many sports have a long history. A form of tennis goes back at least to the medieval period and a game known as camp-ball (a cross between football and handball) was common particularly in East Anglia. Such activities often escalated into violence. By the late sixteenth and early seventeenth centuries football and other popular sports were extremely violent and participation often resulted in physical injury or even death. A number of sports such as cockfighting, archery, prize-fights and wrestling were reflections of aggressive masculinity or simulations of warfare.[308] In a boxing match in 1804, a Godmanchester shepherd John Fisher defeated a waterman from Stanground called Fuller. Such was the ferocity of the fight that Fuller died in the ring.[309] This 'rough culture' did not escape criticism. Many people, particularly those in the middle ranks of society, expressed strong moral disapproval of riotous and uncontrolled pleasure. The Society for the Prevention of Cruelty to Animals was founded in 1824 and their work led to the Cruelty to Animals Act of 1835 which suppressed animal-baiting.[310]

Major changes in the history of sport took place in the second half of the nineteenth century in England. Governing bodies were established and the codification of rules facilitated competition, which rapidly became international. The educational changes introduced by the 1870 Act extended opportunities for participation in sport to children throughout society. Local authorities provided tennis courts, cricket pitches and municipal swimming pools that helped to generate interest in sport. Several sports also started to move in a more professional direction. Partisanship and the need to win began to replace amateur ideals of sportsmanship and fair play. Sportsmen began to be paid for their services. Spectator sports emerged and entrepreneurs discovered that money could be made out of people's spare time.[311] This development of commercial sport was linked to a rapid growth of population and an increase in urbanisation.

Football

Godmanchester was too small a place to support professional sport. The origins of Godmanchester Rovers Football Club are no longer entirely clear. It has been suggested that the club was established in 1911 but an early photograph of 'Godmanchester football team' by Alfred Hendrey is dated 1903. By 2002 the club had reached the Eastern Counties Football League Division One. The highest position it has reached in this league was a creditable 7th place in 2003/4. In 2010/11 Rovers qualified through to the second round proper of the national FA Vase competition by defeating Framlington Town 4-0 and Eynesbury Rovers 2-1. They met Stanway Rovers but were defeated 1-0. Locally the club progressed to the Quarter Final of the Hunts Senior Cup in 2004/5 before losing narrowly by 1-0 to Yaxley. In 2009/10 Godmanchester Rovers had its most successful FA Cup run in its history. They defeated Haverhill 1-0 in the Extra Preliminary Round and after the game, Godmanchester's delighted manager, David Hurst commented, 'I knew if we reproduced the form we showed on Saturday we could take them close to beating them. It's nice to make a bit of history for the club.' Further success in the preliminary round saw Godmanchester defeat Rothwell Corinthians 3-0. In the First Round Qualifying they finally met their match when they went down 2-1 to Northampton Spencer.

Godmanchester Rovers competes against clubs that represent much larger towns such as Great Yarmouth and Clacton so raising money to keep up is a continual challenge. Every year the club has managed to attract top football personalities to their annual dinner including Emlyn Hughes, Nobby Stiles, Paul Merson and Barry Fry. The Rovers' home ground is at Bearscroft Lane on the edge of town. Chairman Keith Gabb has continued to drive the club forwards and in 2009 a new stand and dug outs were installed.

Godmanchester Football Team 1903[312]

Cricket

Competitive cricket in Godmanchester has a long history. In 1903 Godmanchester Cricket Club were the winners of the Smith Barry Cricket Cup. Godmanchester Town Cricket Club is located at the Parks off Fox Grove. It is the leading cricket club in Huntingdonshire and the surrounding areas providing competitive cricket for all standards. For several years the 1st XI has competed in the prestigious East Anglian Premier League. Godmanchester Town were runners up in the league in 2007 but in 2009 finished in last place after winning just four games and were relegated. Triumph followed despair when Godmanchester Town were crowned ECB Indoor Six-a-Side National Club champions in 2010. More than 700 clubs entered the competition but Godmanchester won the title for the first time in their history after beating Poole at Lord's.

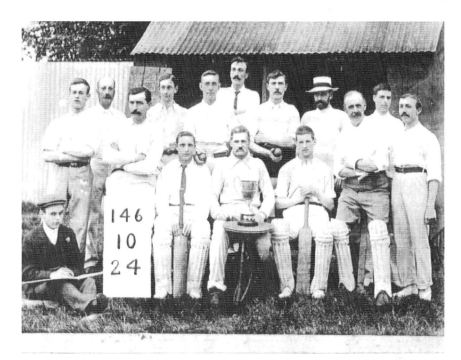

J. Looker, A. W. Brawn, H. Pratt, H. Greening, F. Richards, Rev. F. G. Walker, C. Hunnybun,
E. Abbott, T. Saunders, S. Hunt J. Hopkins, Rev. A. Sloman, H. Sloman, A. Brawn, G. C. Linnage,

Godmanchester Cricket Club 1903[313]

Godmanchester Cricket Club

Bowls

Bowls has a long history and has been played in England from at least the thirteenth century. Originally bowls were usually made of stone and players would aim them towards their target. In Godmanchester, the Royal Oak Bowls Club began in 1929 when play took place on the lawn at the Chestnuts in West Street. But in 1930 the club moved to its present site at the rear of Royal Oak Pub. Bowls in Godmanchester originally was for men only but finally the men relented and admitted women to the club. Throughout its history the club's activities have not been confined to bowls and have included social events such as club dinners and their prize presentation buffet dance. One of the highlights of the year is the open Bowls Competition which takes place during Gala Week.

A number of other sports are enjoyed in Godmanchester. Godmanchester Tennis Club plays on Godmanchester School's floodlit courts and adults of all standards participate. The golf society is based at *The Exhibition* on London Road. The society provides the opportunity for people to play competitive golf without the need to join a golf club.

The Great Ouse has also been a site for sporting and leisure activities. Fishing has long been enjoyed by the town's residents and the Angling Society preserves that tradition both for locals and for visitors. However in 1895 the river froze with ice eight inches thick. Ice skaters enjoyed the opportunity of skating on the river. In February 1895 an ice carnival was held. Mr Hendrey was responsible for the illuminations and assisted by Messrs Brudenell, Markham and Goodliff, lights were arranged along the river. One illumination spelled out, 'Huntingdon and Godmanchester Ice Carnival 1895' but sadly this could not be lit due to lack of candles. Lamps were lit on the bridge and scores of Chinese lanterns were suspended from wires strung across the river near the railway bridge. The carnival started at 7.30 pm. and crowds gathered along the river. Those taking part were mostly in fancy dress and wore masks. A band played, refreshments were served and the highlight was fireworks and rockets.[314]

Sport and leisure continued to be prohibited on Sundays as Sabbatarianism still held sway in Godmanchester. In June 1940 the Town Council debated whether the swings on the Recreation Ground should be used on a Sunday. Councillor Kisby could see no harm in children playing on the swings but this view was not supported by the mayor, Alderman Pratt Anderson. The mayor argued in support of the churches that playing on the swings during divine worship was 'the thin end of the wedge'![315]

Although the history of sport in Godmanchester has been largely modest in scope the town has had its share of famous sportsmen. Darren Bent played for Godmanchester Rovers youth side. Although Bent was a keen supporter of Arsenal and had a season-ticket at Highbury, he went on to play for their arch rivals Tottenham and for England. Iwan Thomas is one of the best 400 metre runners that Britain has ever produced and he also hailed from Godmanchester. Iwan became European Champion at both the 400 metres and the 4×400 metres relay in 1998. In the same year he won gold at the Commonwealth Championships at Kuala Lumpur, and gold again at the IAAF World Cup. In recognition of his achievements Iwan was awarded the MBE.

Portholme

The Ouse Valley offers many opportunities for leisure activities and one of the most popular among Godmanchester residents is walking. Portholme offers a perfect setting for enjoying a leisurely stroll. Portholme is strictly in the parish of Brampton but its importance to the people of Godmanchester makes its inclusion in this book essential. It covers some 300 acres although it is now divided into two by the railway line, which runs from King's Cross to Peterborough and the north. For centuries it has been used for hay and then grazed by cattle after the hay harvest. In winter and early spring Portholme is frequently flooded thus providing natural fertilising of its soil.

Cattle grazing on Portholme in the autumn

Portholme (literally town meadow) is one of the largest flood meadows in England and is designated a Site of Special Scientific Interest (SSSI) because of its wildlife. Of particular importance are the restricted dragonfly *Libellula fulva,* grasses such as Yorkshire fog *Holcus lanatus,* and a range of herbs including lady's bedstraw *Galium verum,* pepper saxifrage *Silaum silaus* and great burnet *Sanguisorba officinalis.*

Samuel Pepys recorded in his diary for 1662 that he watched 'the country maids milking their Cowes there and to see with what mirth they all came home together in pomp with their milk and sometimes they have musique to go before them'.[316] Portholme was used as a racecourse in the eighteenth and nineteenth centuries. A grandstand was located on the meadow and the horse racing attracted large crowds.

Portholme and Huntingdon Race Ground (Norris Museum)

In 1909, the year of Bleriot's cross channel flight, local visitors to the air meeting at Doncaster recorded that Portholme would make an ideal aerodrome. The following year James Radley of Bedford brought his three-cylinder Bleriot monoplane to Portholme. His best attempt flying at a height of 40 feet was sixteen and a half miles at an average speed of 42 m.p.h.[317] The flight was witnessed by Bert Brudenell who recorded this testimony at the age of 91 years:

> *I saw this plane on Portholme in 1910 and saw it take to the air after trials. This plane was flown by Mr Radley who flew round this meadow such a short distance...I also worked on the Sopwith Camel in 1916 that was made at a factory at the end of Ferrars Road.*

Flooded... looking towards Portholme

13

GODMANCHESTER PEOPLE

So far we have looked at many facets of Godmanchester life including the economy, changes in population, agriculture and religion but history is primarily about people. This chapter focuses on individuals who have all left their mark upon Godmanchester throughout the centuries. When so many people have contributed to the life of the town it is invidious to make a choice. Survival of source material is a major factor which determines the choice of individuals who lived in the past. We have chosen four church-men, three medical men, two Emmas and a photographer. The chapter concludes with two people who have lived in the town all their lives. We are grateful to Vera Arnold and John Leach for sharing their memories with us.

Four Churchmen
William of Godmanchester
Our knowledge of William of Godmanchester is limited so we owe a great debt to Sir William Dugdale for compiling his monumental *Monasticon Anglicanum* during the years 1655 to 1673. It is a history of the abbeys, monasteries, hospitals, friaries, and cathedral and collegiate churches in England and Wales. Dugdale chronicles 'the good deeds' of William of Godmanchester who was elected the twenty-first Abbot of Ramsey in 1267. William was responsible for many additions to the Abbey's buildings in-cluding a conduit, a cistern and a new Abbot's Hall. He also made a brass image for the tomb of Count Ailwyn, the founder of Ramsey Abbey, which was 'very costly and splendid in guilding'. During 1285, his nineteenth year as Abbot, he contracted the 'palsey' and died just over a year later.

Walter Welles
Dr Walter Welles was a Puritan lecturer. Puritans regarded the Church of England as only half reformed and wished to 'purify' the church. The radi-

cal Puritan clergy adopted various stances. Some remained in the Church of England whilst others became lecturers or became separatists (the newly emerging non-conformist groups). Puritan lecturers preached on market days and at other published times and were supported by the voluntary gifts of Puritans rather than by tithes. Puritan lecturers were suppressed by the bishops and this was one reason that led Cromwell to conclude that bishops were the enemies of God. Dr John Morrill of the University of Cambridge has uncovered an early letter of Cromwell stressing the need to support such lectureships. Godmanchester's Puritan lecturer during the early years of the seventeenth century was Dr Walter Welles. Little is known about him but Dr Greengrass of Sheffield University has uncovered the evidence that has so far come to light.[318] Welles studied in Leiden and was in Godmanchester in the first half of the 1630s. In June 1635 Welles witnessed the will of a Godmanchester gentleman. According to a letter written by Oliver Cromwell in 1636, Welles was a man 'for goodness and industry and ability to do good every way'. Since his arrival in Huntingdonshire, 'the Lord hath by him wrought much good amongst us'. Clearly Cromwell approved of Dr Welles but the extent of his influence on Cromwell's religious thinking remains elusive.

Stephen Marshall

Stephen Marshall, Godmanchester's most famous son, also became a Puritan. Stephen was born around 1595 just four years before the birth of Oliver Cromwell. The son of a Godmanchester glover, he came from a humble background and his family often depended for survival on gleanings from the fields. Yet he rose to become chaplain to the House of Commons during the Civil War and chaplain to King Charles I when the King was held prisoner at both Holmby House, Northamptonshire and at Carisbrooke Castle on the Isle of Wight.

Stephen Marshall, attended the Queen Elizabeth Grammar School where he 'got as much Grammar learning as his poverty and industry would attain to'. While at the school he was probably influenced in his later religious development by his two schoolmasters, William Brabyn and John Symcotts. He went on to study at Emmanuel College, Cambridge, a hotbed for budding Puritan preachers, whose masters and fellows were responsible for appointing the Godmanchester schoolmaster.[319] Marshall took his MA in 1622 and in 1625 he became vicar of Finchingfield in Essex.

Marshall grew very rich due to his marriage to the niece of a baronet and his links with wealthy Essex Puritans.[320] A convinced Puritan, Marshall gradually adopted Presbyterian convictions and became alienated from the Church of England. It was not long before Bishop William Laud, future Archbishop of Canterbury and arch enemy of Puritanism, was on his case. Marshall survived by subtly changing his position and walking a fine line between the need to conform to the Church of England and his Puritan principles.

Marshall's most famous sermon was entitled 'Meroz Cursed' based on the text Jeremiah chapter 48, verse 10:

A curse on him who is lax in doing the Lord's work
Cursed is every one that witholds his hand from shedding of bloud.

The second part of the verse marks an important intellectual shift. The traditional doctrine was that the king was the Lord's anointed and therefore killing the king would be a sin.[321] Marshall reversed the doctrine so that shedding of blood became an obligation. Marshall invoked the words of the prophet Jeremiah, 'Cursed is every one that *witholds* his hand from shedding of bloud' and his whole sermon is against those who sit on the fence. You are either for me or against me.[322] Marshall's final appeal in the sermon was that 'God hath done great things for us but many great things are yet to be done, much rubbish to be overthrown'. Thus on the eve of the civil war Puritanism adopted a militant stance. History was now in the hands of God who could act suddenly and without warning.

Puritanism's military champion, Oliver Cromwell was born in Huntingdon in 1599 and one of its intellectual champions was born in Godmanchester in 1595. Both died within three years of each other, Marshall in 1655 and Cromwell in 1658. Both men shared the distinction of being buried in Westminster Abbey and being dug up again by the mob after the Restoration.[323]

Charles Gray

Charles Gray was vicar of Godmanchester for twenty five years from 1829 to 1854. Two sermons were preached for Charles Gray at his funeral.[324] Both sermons spoke of Charles Gray as a dutiful priest. He visited the sick, consoled the afflicted and guided the ignorant. His earnest wish was to see the church restored and beautified. St Mary's Church provides surviving evidence for his concerns. He organised the erection of the reredos behind the high altar. He gave church plate to the church in the form of a dish and flagon. The flagon was inscribed 'The gift of Charles Gray, M.A., Vicar, to the Parish Church of Godmanchester, A.D. 1834.'[325] The windows in the chancel are dedicated to his memory:

> To the glory of God and in memory of Rev Charles Gray MA for 25 years vicar of Godmanchester, the east window of this church was erected. Died 30 December 1854 aged 55 years.

Tombstone of Charles Gray and family

He is buried close to the church he loved and buried with him is his 18 month old son who died in 1843 and his wife Agnes who died seven years after Charles. Her body was brought back from Brighton where she had been living. The circumstances of her death were recorded by Dr John Baumgartner of Island Hall. Dr John wrote to his son Mowbray that Agnes died from 'an attack of bronchitis, as people now call a cough, invaded with hasty strides her enfeebled frame, and soon had the mastery over it.' She 'is to be laid in our church yard, beside her husband, close to the garden door, which opens to the church yard'.

Three Medical Men

Dr John Baumgartner

We have already encountered Dr John Baumgartner's tomb on the north side of the churchyard.[326] In 1810 John married Philippa Knight daughter of Samuel Knight of Milton Hall and they had thirteen children, ten of whom survived to adulthood. The 'Old Nest' as Island Hall was fondly called was home to this large and interesting family.

Doctor John Baumgartner[327]

John trained in medicine at Edinburgh University. John's entry in the Baumgartner family tree includes the laudatory description that he was known for "benevolence and unostentatious Acts of Charity". He held clinics for the local poor in his mews and later became one of the founders of the old County Hospital in Huntingdon (now Millfield Court). Dr John Baumgartner lived to be 96 despite (or maybe because of!) his habit of regularly swimming round the island, a practice he continued until a few weeks before his death in 1874. Philippa, who lived to be 90, followed him to the grave in 1892. They are both commemorated in the stained glass window over the south aisle altar of the church which was erected by three generations of their family.

Dr Robert Fox

Robert Fox lived for just 45 years but in this relatively short life he achieved a great deal in many fields of scholarly endeavour. Fox trained in medicine and was prominent in the Huntingdonshire Medico-Chirurgical Society. At a meeting of the society the building was struck by lightning and this prompted Fox's study of electricity. He developed a large 'atmospheric battery' which was attached to his house in Post Street for the conduction of lightning. Dr Robert Fox was one of the bailiffs of the borough in 1831–32. He lived to see his vision of a Literary and Scientific Institution in what is now the Commemoration Hall in Huntingdon come to fruition. The grand opening was on 7 September 1842 when 120 people gathered to drink toasts to the project's success. 'A glorious eulogy' was given to Dr Fox, 'the projector of the building'.[328] Fox gave his collection of curiosities and apparatus to the Institution. Robert Fox also researched the history of the town and his history of Godmanchester published in 1831 is an important secondary source for current historians.

Dr John Middlemiss

Like Robert Fox, John Middlemiss was also a medical man with other interests. In his book *Fairground Steam Engines 1864-1934*, Dr John revealed the source of his passion:

> As a child I was fortunate in living in Settle, Yorkshire on the main road from Keighley to Kendal. This meant that road engines and showman's locomotives passed the house often...my fascination with fairground steam is of very long standing.[329]

Few residents can have failed to encounter John Middlemiss for one of the common sights of Godmanchester was Dr John and his steam engine. The Middlemiss family moved to Godmanchester from the north of England in 1968. His steam engine, *The Busy Bee*, took no less than five days to make the journey. John served Godmanchester as a G.P. for many years but he also served the community in some unusual ways. On 11 June 1972, John and his steam engine rescued Doris and John Anderson by using *Busy Bee* in their back garden to power up the lights for their chemist shop's 21st birthday party! No wonder St Mary's Church was packed for his funeral. Middlemiss Close on the new Devana Park development is a permanent reminder of the family.

Two Emmas

Emma Baumgartner

Emma Baumgartner was born in 1828 to Dr John Baumgartner and his wife Philippa of Island Hall. She was one of 13 children; 10 of whom survived to adulthood. Emma was born in Geneva, Switzerland as her paternal grandfather was Swiss and the family still had strong connections with that country. They had spent several years there with their growing family before Emma's birth, but in the autumn of 1829 the family returned to England and Godmanchester. Emma's childhood must have been a noisy, happy one with so many brothers and sisters for company in a riverside home with the advantage of a somewhat overgrown island for solitude if needed. The children were encouraged to join in discussions at home and must have been aware of their doctor father's concern for the welfare of the inhabitants of Godmanchester. As they grew up they continued to visit the continent where their education was supplemented and their horizons widened.

Emma's background may have influenced her later life for she became passionate about helping those less fortunate around her in the town. She cared deeply about education and gave much time and energy to night schools and classes for young men as well as clubs and recreational activities. She taught in the Sunday School and did much visiting in the parish. Her other main concern was the encouragement of temperance and even abstinence in the local community. Emma was also a great supporter of the Salvation Army and in later life tried to set up a temperance hotel with her own financial backing in the old Horseshoe Hotel (now Gatehouse Estate

Agents). Emma was to be disappointed that the plan never came to fruition.

Emma Baumgartner

Emma worked to improve the lives of many of the poorer folk of the town, but her own life was enhanced by fortunate contacts with highly influential people of her time. Her hobby of painting led her to write to John Ruskin for advice. At length he replied with the suggestion she contact a pupil of his, a Miss Octavia Hill who became a life-long friend and undoubtedly encouraged Emma's philanthropic pursuits. Octavia enjoyed visits to Emma at Island Hall and in turn Emma would accompany her friend to such places as the 'Ragged' School in Brick Lane in the East End of London. Octavia Hill became a great social reformer involved in the setting up of social housing and was also a founding member of the National Trust.

Emma never married, but had countless nieces and nephews. She spent her last days living in a house called 'Pomona' (now Heronshaws) in Post Street a few doors away from the 'Old Nest' as the family always called Island Hall. She died in 1911 and is buried on the north side of the graveyard not far from her parents and two of her brothers.

Heronshaws Post Street

Emma Roberts

Born in 1833 in Aldgate, London Emma Roberts is believed to be Godman-chester's first centenarian. Emma remained a spinster and was a member of Godmanchester's Particular Baptist Church. Her hundredth birthday was celebrated by the whole community and became a semi-civic occasion. A collection was made for her in the town and on her birthday, 8 April 1933 the Mace bearer knocked on her cottage door near the church. The Mayor, Mrs Carr, presented her with a scroll with the inscription:

With long life will I satisfy him and show him my salvation.

Presented to Emma Roberts on the occasion of her 100th birthday with the affectionate esteem of many friends and neighbours in the ancient borough of Godmanchester April 8th 1933

She also received a large iced cake, a basket of flowers and a purse containing money from the town collection. Emma lived to the age of 103 and on the day of her funeral the boys from the Queen Elizabeth School were given special permission to watch the procession pass by School Hill.

Alfred Hendrey

Alfred was born in 1853, the youngest of six children. Like his father Fuller Hendrey, Alfred began work as a fishmonger but soon started to develop his interest as an amateur photographer. In 1859 he moved to 52 Post Street where he acquired a studio. He advertised his services as a photographer specialising in portraits and landscapes. Business prospered and he opened further studios in St Ives and Ramsey. The highlight of his career was being invited to photograph the visit of Edward VII on a visit to the Earl of Sandwich at Hinchingbrooke House in 1906. He died at the relatively young age of 56 in 1910 as a result of committing suicide by taking poison. Despite his sad end, Hendrey left an enduring legacy of Godmanchester photographs which are a priceless source of information about the late nineteenth and early twentieth centuries.

Vera Arnold

Vera was born in 1916 in New Street, the ninth of fourteen children and has lived in Godmanchester all her life. At four years old, Vera went to St Anne's School, a mixed infants and girls only junior school. It stood on the site where Woodley Court is now situated. Apart from basic subjects, the girls were taught needlework and domestic skills and for recreation, netball. One of her earliest memories was of the headmistress Miss Hesscroft. Miss Hesscroft was a very tall lady and nervous of falling during heavy snow during one particularly adverse winter. Vera and Joan Makey used to escort the headmistress from her house in The Causeway to the school each morning. They were rewarded with tea at her home. Vera's teachers included Mrs Sawyer (Infants) Mrs Wilderspin (ages 6-7), Miss Ashley (Minnie Hall) and Doris Gilson (Juniors). Doris Gilson would accompany the girls into the river when they learned to swim from the bathing area opposite Island Hall. There were separate changing rooms for boys and girls and the steps down into the river may still be seen. A particular memory was of the flower shows that were held at Farm Hall when it was owned by the Towgoods prior to the war.

Life was not easy for Vera's family and the church contributed to their wellbeing in a number of ways. A notable occasion was the annual Sunday School outing when hordes of children would go by train to Skegness for the day. Vera's family also belonged to a number of church clubs and Vera took the money each week to the Dewsbury sisters at the church rooms: 6d for clothing and a shilling for coal. When the cards were full they were exchanged for goods. A full coal card resulted in the delivery of a ton of coal and one year her mother had a new coat from the clothing card.

During the Second World War Vera was employed in Domestic Service on Offord Hill but left to do 'war work' which was employment in the Brewery in Huntingdon! Vera remembers the bomb dropping in Cow Lane and a number of street parties that were held to commemorate victory.

John Leach

John was born in the 1940s. His mother was a Thoday and long before John was born, Grandfather Thoday was the caretaker of the bathing place and the old water mill which stood at the end of Mill Yard car park. At that time it was no longer in use and due to its derelict state of repair was eventually demolished. Mill Yard was not the empty space it is now, but was bordered by cottages both at the front on Post Street and along the high wall separating the yard from Island Hall. John was one of 7 children and he recounts a very different childhood from that of most children today. It reflects a greater freedom to roam with friends away from parental intervention which suited John well as he was always up to mischief of some kind and on the look out to earn pocket money. One way was being a choir boy at the parish church where he was paid to sing at funerals and weddings. Along with his brothers, he went to both services on a Sunday and also afternoon Sunday School. The long sermons were hard to bear for active boys like John and they risked being 'torn off a strip' by the vicar, Rev Edwards, for talking and sucking mints. The organist Mollie Crouch was also a force to be reckoned with! John particularly remembers Oscar George, an adult choir member, for his beautiful voice which carried over the other voices.

Another adult in the choir was Dr Sears whom John remembers for his concern and kindness especially to local boys like himself. Dr Sears obviously understood that the energy and exuberance of boys needed to be channelled so each summer he organised camps at Gamlingay where between 30 and 40 boys could camp under canvas for several weeks. The boys travelled from Godmanchester in Mr Pettit's lorry and paid 10s a week for their food, to work on a farm owned by Dr Ellis, but they also had plenty of free time for such activities as making camp fires. It was a great shock when Dr Sears died in his forties, but he is still fondly remembered not only as a skilled doctor at the old Huntingdon County Hospital, but as a man devoted to the local lads.

Another person involved with the local youth was Mr Parcell, a council surveyor who lived at Dial House in Cambridge Road. He ran the Boy Scout group which used to meet at the Liberal Hall where Dr Sears' club also met. It was in Post Street opposite the Queen Elizabeth School. There was also a boxing club held in the Queen Elizabeth School run by Mr Moffatt the dentist and Ted Cooper. Boxing tournaments were organised with local clubs by Bert Twigden.

John remembers boys and girls taking part in fishing contests along the river over the Chinese Bridge. This was followed by prize giving and tea in the Church Hall. May Day was a wonderful day for children and adults alike especially if the sun shone. It was celebrated in the grounds of Farm Hall along West Street and people were entertained by a silver band as well as dancing round the maypole. There were plenty of treats in the form of candy floss, toffee apples, ices, tea and cakes as well as stalls selling home-made cakes and jams. November 5th was also a memorable time when together with his brothers and friends, John built a very large bonfire on the meadow at the back of Toll Bar Cottages on the Avenue.

14

CONTINUITY AND CHANGE

The history of Godmanchester can only be understood by studying it in a wider context. The most important events in Godmanchester's history had their origins elsewhere in the world. The first humans who arrived in Godmanchester were descended from the first *homo sapiens* who evolved in Africa. People were forced by the ice sheets to retreat from these islands but they returned to the Ouse Valley from Europe. The first century occupation was the result of the political ambitions of Claudius in Rome. Climate change and cattle plague in central Europe led to the famine of the early fourteenth century. The Black Death had its origins in either Southern Russia or perhaps further East. Christianity, which displaced the earlier religions of Godmanchester, came from the Middle East. Changes to Christian belief and practice in Godmanchester were shaped by Henry VIII's conflict with the Pope in Rome and Darwin's discoveries in the Galapagos Islands.

Today Godmanchester's links with the wider world are ever more extensive. Many residents commute to London and elsewhere to work. They shop not just locally in Huntingdon and at regional shopping centres such as Cambridge and Peterborough but from far and wide on the internet. Goods are delivered to Godmanchester from around the world. Godmanchester's links with Europe are reflected in its twinning arrangements with three towns: Wertheim in Baden-Württemberg, Szentendre on the River Danube north of Budapest and Salon De Provence, a commune in the Bouches-du-Rhone in southern France. Even religious worship is no longer purely local. Some people travel into Godmanchester to worship at its parish church because they like the style of worship. Others travel to worship in the opposite direction to other parishes because they do not.

Geography was decisive in the development of Godmanchester's history. Mesolithic people were drawn to the area because it is situated on a river valley which provided a rich source of food. The early Neolithic farmers enjoyed the luxury of its easy-to-work soil. The Romans built a fort here because it was the crossroads of two major roads and the site of the crossing of the River Ouse. More recently, the building of the A14 road has had a major impact on the town. The road has brought not just an enormous increase in traffic and the frustrations of congestion but new industries to the town.

For centuries, Godmanchester has been a typical English country market town. Its economy was largely dependent on agriculture but it was also a place of marketing and exchange with tradesmen and craftsmen plying their wares. It was a relatively prosperous town, neither located in one of the richest counties of the south of England nor among the poorest in the north. Economic changes have meant that the town's inhabitants are no longer principally employed in agriculture. The industrial revolution may have been based in other parts of the country such as Lancashire and West Yorkshire but its products transformed the lives of Godmanchester people. In the seventeenth century even Godmanchester's better-off labourers owned little more than the clothes that they stood up in, their bed, a single sheet and a few pots and pans. By the late eighteenth century a new world was dawning. The population owned so many more goods and items such as clocks were commonly owned even by labourers. A consumer revolution had begun which was to come to fruition in the twentieth century.

The enormous changes in society over the last 150 years are highlighted by an examination of births, marriages and deaths in Huntingdonshire. In the year 1863, there were 2,090 births in the county of which just 139 (7 per cent) were outside of marriage. Only 73 (18 per cent) of 412 marriages were not solemnised in the Church of England. There were 1,373 deaths of which 562 (41 per cent) were aged under 5 years old but only 32 (2 per cent) aged over 85 years. By contrast today more than 40 per cent of births are outside of marriage and only 24 per cent of marriages take place in the Church of England. Now 36 per cent of all deaths in England are people aged 85 years and over and less than 1 per cent of deaths are children under 5 years old.

In the last four decades the population of Godmanchester has risen rapidly. There were still only just over 3,000 people living here in 1971 whereas now the population exceeds 6,000. The ethnicity of its people has also changed significantly in just the last ten years. Average house prices in Godmanchester have risen by more than 1,500 per cent since 1974 so that by 2010 the average house in Godmanchester costs more than £200,000. The rising real cost of housing has not reduced demand and new housing developments have been built to house the much larger population.

Despite all the massive changes there is still continuity. The legacy of the past still leaves its mark on the town. The road system in the centre of Godmanchester follows the path of the Roman walls. Godmanchester is still surrounded by arable land and vestiges of the medieval ridge and furrow field system can be seen in the middle of the town cricket pitch. In the twelfth century, Henry Archdeacon of Huntingdon recorded in his *Historia Anglorum* that Godmanchester was an attractive town with a beautiful and splendid site. Most of the inhabitants would still agree that Godmanchester remains a much loved and unique community.

Sunset at Godmanchester

END NOTES

CHAPTER 2: THE FIRST HUMANS IN BRITAIN

[1] C. Zimmer, *Smithsonian intimate guide to human origins*, (Collins: New York, 2005) p.112.

[2] Stringer, *Homo Britannicus*, p.132.

[3] Stringer, *Homo Britannicus*, p.135.

[4] From the Midland Railway Pit, Buckden; grid ref. 210690.

[5] V. Gaffney, S. Fitch and D. Smith, *Europe's lost world: the rediscovery of Doggerland*, (Council for British Archaeology: York, 2009) p.111.

[6] Stringer, *Homo Britannicus*, pp.149-57.

[7] Gaffney *et al.*, *Europe's lost world*, p.43.

CHAPTER 3: GODMANCHESTER'S BEGINNINGS

[8] Gaffney *et al.*, *Europe's lost world*, p.45.

[9] T. Reynolds, 'The Mesolithic' in T. Kirby and S. Oosthuizen (eds.) *An Atlas of Cambridgeshire and Huntingdonshire History*, (Anglia Polytechnic University: Cambridge, 2000) p.6.

[10] Stringer, *Homo Britannicus*, p.215.

[11] M. Parker Pearson, *Bronze Age Britain*, (Batsford: London, 2005) pp.9-22.

[12] D. Stocker, *The English Landscape; The East Midlands*, (Collins: London, 2006) p.116.

[13] J. Pollard, 'The Neolithic' in T. Kirby and S. Oosthuizen (eds.) *An Atlas of Cambridgeshire and Huntingdonshire History*, (Anglia Polytechnic University: Cambridge, 2000) p.7.

[14] Pollard, 'The Neolithic', p.7.

[15] F. McAvoy, 'The development of a Neolithic monument complex at Godmanchester, Cambridgeshire' in M. Dawson, (ed.), *Prehistoric, Roman, and post-Roman landscapes of the Great Ouse Valley*, (Council for British Archaeology: York, 2000) p.119.

[16] B. Galloway, *History of Cambridgeshire*, (Phillimore: Chichester, 1983) p.16.

[17] T. Malim, *Stonea and the Roman fens*, (Tempus: Stroud, 2005) p.31.

[18] C. Haselgrove, 'The Iron Age' in J. Hunter and I. Ralston (eds.) *The Archaeology of Britain: An Introduction from the Upper Palaeolithic to the Industrial Revolution*, (Routledge: London, 1999) p.125.

[19] M. Hinman, *Bob's Wood, the Story so far: An introduction to the Hinchingbrooke excavations*, (Cambridgeshire County Council: Cambridge, 2003).

[20] S. James and V. Rigby, *Britain and the Celtic Iron Age*, (British Museum Press: London, 1997) p.75.

[21] Malim, *Stonea and the Roman fens*, p.40.

[22] J. Creighton, *Britannia: the creation of a Roman Province*, (Routledge:Abingdon, 2006) p.20.

[23] G. Webster, *The Roman invasion of Britain*, (Routledge: London, 1993) p.49.

[24] Norris Museum, St Ives, Cambridgeshire, catalogue number X1104.

[25] R. Niblett, *Verulamium: the Roman city of St Albans* (Tempus: Stroud, 2001) p.52.

[26] N. Faulkner, *The Decline and Fall of Roman Britain* (Tempus: Stroud, 2000) pp.18-19.

[27] G. De La Bedoyere, *Defying Rome*, (Tempus: Stroud, 2003) pp.60-2.

[28] F. Pryor, *Britain in the Middle Ages: an archaeological history* (Harper: London, 2006) p.2.

[29] A. Jones, *Settlement, burial and industry in Roman Godmanchester* (Birmingham University Field Archaeology Unit: Birmingham, 2003) p.169.

[30] Durovigutum means literally a thriving strongpoint.

[31] A fallen voussoir from the central carriageway uncovered during the 1972/3 excavations showed that the wall finish was of rusticated limestone ashlar.

[32] *Daily Telegraph* Obituary 11 Aug 2005.

[33] The dig was featured on the popular Channel Four archaeology programme, *Time Team* shown on 9 April 2006.

[34] T. Phillips, *Roman remains at 8 New Street, Godmanchester, Cambridgeshire*, (CAM ARC: Cambridge, 2007) p.2.

[35] P. Bigmore, *The Bedfordshire and Huntingdonshire Landscape*, (Hodder and Stoughton: London, 1979) p.46.

[36] Jones, *Settlement, burial and industry*, p.170.

[37] J. Wacher, *Roman Britain*, (Dent: London, 1978) p129; G. De La Bedoyere, *Roman Towns in Britain*, (Batsford: London, 1992) p.108.

[38] Faulkner, *The decline and fall of Roman Britain*, p.60.

[39] A. Taylor, 'Roman industry' in T. Kirby and S. Oosthuizen (eds.) *An Atlas of Cambridgeshire and Huntingdonshire History*, (Anglia Polytechnic University: Cambridge, 2000) 15.

[40] Malim, *Stonea and the Roman fens*, pp.156-8 and p.199.

[41] Jones, *Settlement, burial and industry*, p.170.

[42] Faulkner, *The decline and fall of Roman Britain*, p.67.

[43] Malim, *Stonea and the Roman fens*, p.214.

[44] D. Perring, *The Roman House in Britain*, (Routledge: London, 2002) p.181.

[45] Malim, *Stonea and the Roman fens*, p.214.

[46] A. Taylor, 'A Roman burial at Godmanchester', *Records of Huntingdonshire* (1993) 28-33, p.33.

[47] M. Green, 'The figurines' *Records of Huntingdonshire* (1993) 33-35, p.33.

[48] Malim, *Stonea and the Roman fens*, p.158.

[49] Jones, *Settlement, burial and industry*, p.2.

[50] Jones, *Settlement, burial and industry*, p.30

[51] Jones, *Settlement, burial and industry*, p.35.

CHAPTER 4: FROM THE EARLY MEDIEVAL PERIOD TO THE CHARTER

[52] B. Yorke, *The conversion of Britain*, (Pearson Longman: Harlow, 2006) p. 44.

[53] Malim, *Stonea and the Roman fens*, p.158. The Huntingdonshire hundred entitled Hurstingstone may be an echo of the local tribe known as the 'Hyrstingas'.

[54] B. Yorke, 'The origins of Mercia' in M. P. Brown and C. A. Farr (eds.) *Mercia: an Anglo-Saxon Kingdom in Europe*, (Leicester University Press: Leicester, 2001) p.20.

[55] D. Banham, 'Food and Drink' in M. Lapidge *et al* (eds.) *Anglo Saxon Encyclopaedia*, (Blackwell: Oxford, 2000) pp.190-1.

[56] H. Hamerow, 'Hamwic' *British Archaeology* August 2002 http://www.britarch.ac.uk/ba/ba66/feat3.shtml last accessed 2 June 2010.

[57] F. Pryor, *Britain in the Middle Ages: an archaeological history* (Harper: London, 2006) p. 63.

[58] Lesley Webster, former keeper of the department of prehistory at the British Museum, Sunday BBC Radio 4, 27 September 2009.

[59] G. Seddon, *Cardinal West, Godmanchester, Cambridgeshire*, (Hertfordshire Archaeological Trust: Hertford, 2000) p.2.

[60] R. Mortimer, *Mill Common, Huntingdon, Cambridgeshire*, (Cambridgeshire County Council AFU: Cambridge, 2006) p.6.

[61] D. Hadley, 'Invisible Vikings' *British Archaeology* 64 (2002) 16-21.

[62] B. Yorke, *Wessex in the early Middle Ages*, (Leicester University Press: Leicester, 1995) p.105.

[63] J. Parker, *England's Darling: the Victorian Cult of Alfred the Great*, (Manchester University Press: Manchester, 2007) p.ix.

[64] B. Yorke, 'The Most Perfect Man in History?' *History Today*, Vol. 49 (1999) 8-14.

[65] M. Hinman, *Prehistoric and Roman activity at the new school site, London Road, Godmanchester: an archaeological evaluation*, (Fulbourn, 1996) pp.3-4.

[66] A. Woodger, 'The Danes in Huntingdonshire' in *Records of Huntingdonshire* Vol.2 (1990) 27-29, p.27.

[67] C. Dyer, *Making a living in the Middle Ages*, (Yale University Press: New Haven, 2002) p.82.

[68] C. Hart, 'The hidation of Huntingdonshire', *Proceedings of the Cambridge Antiquarian Society*, vol. 61 (1968), 55-66.

[69] M. Bailey, 'Villeinage in England' *Economic History Review* Vol. 62 (2009) 430-457, p.433.

[70] Dyer, *Making a living in the Middle Ages*, p.74.

[71] Most references to monetary values in this book are cited in pre-decimal sterling (pounds, shillings and pence), in which:12 old pence (styled as 12*d.*) =1 shilling (1*s.*) = 5 new pence (5p); and 20 shillings (20*s.*) = £1; thus £1 6*s.* 8*d.* = £1.34.

[72] M. Jurkowski, C. Smith and D. Crook, *Lay taxes in England and Wales 1188-1688*, (PRO Publications: London, 1998) p.7

[73] D. Danziger and G. Gillingham, *The year of Magna Carta* (Coronet: London, 2003) p.183.

[74] W. Warren, *King John* (Yale: New Haven, 1997) p.199.

[75] D. A. Carpenter, *The struggle for mastery: Britain 1066-1284* (Penguin: London, 2003) p.270.

[76] Reginald son of Robert served for less than a month in 1280. He was replaced by William Manipenny on 27 June 1280. J. A. Raftis, *A small town in late medieval England: Godmanchester 1278-1400*, (Pontifical Institute of Medieval Studies: Toronto, 1982) pp.61ff.

[77] M. Green, *Godmanchester* (Oleander Press: Cambridge, 1977) pp. 29 and 39.

CHAPTER 5: WHO WERE THE PEOPLE?

[78] Greene, *Godmanchester*, p.10.

[79] Stocker, *The English Landscape*, p.52.

[80] J. R. Maddicott, 'Plague in England in the seventh century' Past and Present 156, 1997, 7-54; C. J. Arnold, 'Stress as a stimulus for socio-economic change: Anglo Saxon England in the seventh century' in C. Renfrew and S. Shennan, (eds.) Ranking, Resource, and Exchange (CUP: Cambridge, 1982) p.127.

[81] Bede, *The Ecclesiastical History of the English Nation From the Coming of Julius Caesar Into This Island in the 60th Year Before the Incarnation of Christ Till the Year of Our Lord 731, Book III* (University of Michigan Press: Ann Arbor, 2009)

[82] K. Manchester, 'Diseases' in M. Lapidge *et al.*, (eds.) *Anglo Saxon Encyclopaedia* (OUP: Oxford, 2000) p.142.

[83] R. Bartlett, *England under the Norman and Angevin kings, 1075-1225* (OUP: Oxford, 2002) pp.290-2.

[84] S. Rigby, 'Urban population in late medieval England: the evidence of the lay subsidies', *Economic History Review* Vol. 63, (2010), 393-417, p.393.

[85] B. M.S. Campbell, *Land and people in medieval England* (Ashgate: Aldershot, 2009) p.11.

[86] Public Record Office, SC5/Hunts/Tower/1.

[87] S. Raban, *A Second Domesday?: The Hundred Rolls of 1279-80*, (OUP: Oxford, 2004) p.51.

[88] S. Raban, 'The Making of the 1279–80 Hundred Rolls', *Historical Research*, Vol. 70, pp.123-145.

[89] B. Campbell, 'Benchmarking medieval economic development: England, Wales, Scotland and Ireland, c.1290' *Economic History Review*, Vol.61 (2008), 896-945 p.926.

[90] D, Hey, *The Oxford Companion to Local and Family History* (OUP: Oxford, 1996) p.341.

[91] Huntingdonshire Archives HP/34/5/2

[92] K. Tiller, *English Local History: An Introduction* (Sutton, Stroud, 2002) p.164.

[93] T. Arkell, 'Identifying regional variations from the hearth tax', *The Local Historian*, 33, (2003) p.148.

[94] Hey, *Oxford Companion to Local and Family History*, p.341.

[95] P. J. Corfield, 'East Anglia' in P. Clark (ed.) *The Cambridge Urban History of Britain Vol. II* (CUP: Cambridge,) p.46.

[96] K. Wrightson, *English society, 1580-1680* (Routledge: London, 2003) p.31.

[97] J. Bedells, 'The gentry of Huntingdonshire', in *Local Population Studies*, 44, (1990) pp.35-6.

[98] W. Harrison, *Description of England* (Folger Shakespeare Library: Washington, 1968) p.114.

[99] E. Rimbault, (ed.), *The miscellaneous works in prose and verse of Sir Thomas Overbury*, (J R Smith: London, 1856) p.149.

[100] P. Laslett, *The world we have lost-further explored*, (Routledge: London, 1983), p.44.

[101] G. Markham, *The English Husbandman* (London, 1613) p.a3.

[102] J. A. Sharpe, *Early modern England; a social history 1550-1760* 2nd edn (Arnold: London, 1997) p.208.

[103] Wrightson, *English society*, p.40.

[104] K. Wrightson, *Earthly necessities* (Penguin: New Haven, 2000) p.34.

[105] B. Coward, *Social change and continuity*, (Longman: Harlow, 1997) p.56.

[106] Wrightson, *Earthly necessities*, p.307.

[107] Laslett, *The world we have lost-further explored*, p.32.

[108] Wrightson, *English society*, p.41.

[109] G. Clark, 'The long march of history: farm wages, population, and economic growth, England 1200-1869' *Economic History Review*, LX (2007), p.132.

[110] Clark, 'The long march of history' p.100.

[111] Dyer, *Making a living in the Middle Ages*, pp.280-1.

[112] L. Weatherill, *Consumer behaviour and material culture*, (Routledge: London, 1996) pp.209-212; V. Brodsky Elliott, 'Mobility and marriage in pre-industrial England' (unpublished Ph.D. thesis, University of Cambridge, 1979).

[113] M. Overton, *Agricultural revolution in England* (CUP: Cambridge, 1996) p.38.

[114] A. Fletcher and J., Stevenson, *Order and disorder in early modern England* (CUP: Cambridge, 1985) p.1.

[115] D. Spaeth, *The church in an age of danger: parsons and parishioners 1660-1740* (CUP: Cambridge, 2000) p.7.

[116] A. Flather, T*he politics of place: a study of church seating in Essex c.1580-1640* (Friends of the Department of English Local History: Leicester, 1999) pp.25 and 54.

[117] K Thomas, *The ends of life* (OUP: Oxford, 2009) p.116.

[118] T. Arkell, 'Identifying regional variations from the hearth tax', *The Local Historian*, 33 (2003), p.148.

CHAPTER 6: THE ECONOMY

[119] B.M.S. Campbell, 'The Land' in R Horrox and W.M. Ormrod (eds.) A *Social History of England*, (CUP: Cambridge, 2006) p.179.

[120] Bigmore, *The Bedfordshire and Huntingdonshire Landscape*, p.211.

[121] Dredge was a cash crop that could be malted for ale.

[122] West, East, Basscroft, Forest, Depden and East Garden Field; Green, *Godmanchester* p.34.

[123] B. Campbell, 'Nature as historical protagonist: environment and society in pre-industrial England', *Economic History Review*, Vol. 63, (2010) 281-314, pp.284-291.

[124] Dyer, *Making a living in the Middle Ages*, pp.278-79.

[125] S. King and G. Timmins, *Making sense of the industrial revolution: English economy and society 1700-1850* (Manchester University Press: Manchester, 2001) p. 165.

[126] A. Kussmaul, *A General View of the Rural Economy of England 1538-1840*, (CUP: Cambridge, 1993) pp.1-4.

[127] A figure of 100 implies an average level of marriages so Kimbolton's 193 in the autumn months show that marriage levels were almost double the norm.

[128] Campbell, 'The Land', p.202.

[129] Priv. Act of Parl. 43 George III cap. 3 (Jamison, 1932) p.286.

[130] J. Humphries, 'Enclosure common rights and women: the proletarianisation of families in the late eighteenth and early nineteenth centuries' *Journal of Economic History*, 1990.

[131] E. Evans, *The Forging of the Modern State*, (Longman: London, 1996) p.156.

[132] E.g. KHCP/1/14/1; KHCP/1/14/2.

[133] M. Turner, 'Agriculture' in R. Floud and P. Johnson (eds.) *The Cambridge Economic History of Modern Britain Volume II* (CUP: Cambridge, 2004) pp.133-160.

[134] R. Perren, *Agriculture in Depression* (CUP: Cambridge, 1995) p.7.

[135] P. J. Perry, 'Where was the 'Great Agricultural Depression'? A Geography of Agricultural Bankruptcy in Late Victorian England and Wales *Agricultural History Review* XX (1972), 30-45.

[136] G. Boyer, 'Living standards 1860-1939' in R. Floud and P. Johnson (eds.) *The Cambridge Economic History of Modern Britain Volume II* (CUP: Cambridge, 2004) p.281.

[137] I. B. Hunter, *Huntingdonshire 1940-1998 revisited*, (Private publication: Undated)

[138] Raftis, *A small town in late medieval England*, p.135.

[139] Overton, *Agricultural revolution in England*, p.36.

[140] W. Page, G. Proby and S. Inskip Ladds, 'Parishes: Godmanchester', in *A History of the County of Huntingdon: Volume 2* Victoria County History 1932 p.291.

[141] D. Crossley, *Post-Medieval archaeology in Britain* (Leicester, 1990) p.71.

[142] J. De Vries, *The economy of Europe* in an age of crisis (CUP: Cambridge, 1976) p.187.

[143] H. Mui and L. Mui, *Shops and shopkeeping in eighteenth-century England* (Routledge: London, 1989) pp.40 and 295-97.

[144] Carter, 'An urban society and its hinterland', p.12.

[145] M. Carter, *Edmund Pettis' survey of St Ives, 1728*, (Cambridgeshire Records Society: Cambridge, 2002) p.32.

[146] Danziger and Gillingham, *1215: The year of Magna Carta*, p.48.

[147] Green, *Godmanchester* p.41.

[148] I. Mortimer, *The Time Travellers Guide to Medieval England*, (Bodley Head: London, 2008) p.128.

[149] C. Dunn, *The Book of Huntingdon*, (Quotes Ltd: Chesham, 1977) p.47

[150] Stocker, *The English Landscape*, p.211.

[151] I. Mortimer, *The Perfect King: The Life of Edward III, Father of the English Nation*, (Jonathan Cape: London, 2006) p. 460.

[152] C. Dyer, *An age of transition*, (OUP: Oxford, 2007) pp.23-24.

[153] D. Bogart, 'Turnpike Trusts and property income' *Economic History Review* Vol. 62 (2009) 128-152, p.128.

[154] M. Frearson, 'Transportation in early modern Cambridgeshire and Huntingdonshire' in T. Kirby and S. Oosthuizen (eds.) *An Atlas of Cambridgeshire and Huntingdonshire History* (Anglia Polytechnic University: Cambridge, 2000) 46.

[155] M.P. Carter, 'Town or urban society? St Ives in Huntingdonshire, 1630-1740', in C. Phythian-Adams (ed.) *Societies, cultures and kinship*, (Leicester University Press: London, 1993) p.79.

[156] Jamison, 1932 p286

[157] F. W. Bird, *Memorials of Godmanchester*, (Peterborough Advertiser Company: Peterborough, 1911) XVII.

[158] Wrigley, 'Urban growth and agricultural change', p. 49; Corfield, *Impact of English Towns*, p.70; J., M., Ellis *The Georgian Town*, (Palgrave: Basingstoke, 2001) p.45; Sharpe, *Early modern England*, p.88.

[159] D. Bogart, 'Turnpike Trusts and property income: new evidence on the effects of transport improvements and legislation in eighteenth-century England' *Economic History Review* Vol. 62 No. 1 (2009) 128-152, p.150.

[160] Dunn, *The Book of Huntingdon*, p.48.

[161] Pigot's Directory 1830.

[162] L. Oppitz, *East Anglia Railways Remembered*, (Newbury: Countryside Books, 1989) p.54.

[163] V. Mitchell, K. Smith, C. Awdry and A. Mott, *Branch Lines around Huntingdon: Kettering to Cambridge*, (Middleton Press: Midhurst, 1991) p.65.

[164] R. Burn-Murdoch, 'The tracks of my tears' *Hunts Post* 3 June 2009 pp.28-9.

[165] J. Morris, *Travels with Virginia Woolf*, (Pimlico: London, 1997) pp.77-80.

[166] The site is clearly identified on E. M. M. Good's map of 1853, Huntingdonshire Archives, ACC 2032.

[167] Hansard *HC Deb 22 June 1939 vol. 348 cc2485-6W*

[168] *Hunts Post* 13 May 1905.

[169] *Hunts Post* 3 October 1908 p.8 column 6.

[170] *Hunts Post* 4 December 1909, p.4 column 7.

[171] *Hunts Post* 25 August 1916 p.1.

[172] 2001 Census.

CHAPTER 7: RELIGION

[173] R. Hutton, *The pagan religions of the ancient British Isles*, (Wiley Blackwell: Oxford, 1993) pp.1-2.

[174] W. Uttal, *Dualism*, (Routledge: London, 2004) p.49.

[175] Zimmer, *Smithsonian intimate guide to human origins*, p.112.

[176] Zimmer, *Smithsonian intimate guide to human origins*, p.121.

[177] *World's oldest ritual discovered. Worshipped the python 70,000 years ago*, published 2 December 2006 http://www.apollon.uio.no/vis/art/2006_4/Artikler/python_english last accessed 8 Feb 2009.

[178] The original bronze plaque was found with late third-century rubbish in the disused aqueduct of the baths of the mansio, at present-day No. 2 Pinfold Lane, grid ref. 245704; Cambridgeshire County Council Sites and Monuments Record, SMR 928.

[179] A. Taylor, 'Roman Religion' in T. Kirby and S. Oosthuizen (eds.) *Atlas of Cambridgeshire and Huntingdonshire History*, (Anglia Polytechnic University: Cambridge, 2000) p.18.

[180] S. Price and E. Kearns, *The Oxford Dictionary of Classical Myth and Religion*, (OUP: Oxford, 2003) p. 345.

[181] The figurine of the goddess Venus was found in second-century rubbish pits outside the north-east wall of the mansio, at present-day No. 2 Pinfold Lane, grid ref. 245704.

[182] T. Phillips, *Roman remains at 8 New Street, Godmanchester, Cambridgeshire*, (CAM ARC: Cambridge, 2007) p.30.

[183] Donatists were those who believed that the church should only consist of the pure, not those who had fallen into sin.

[184] D. Petts, *Christianity in Roman Britain*, (Tempus: Stroud, 2003) pp.55, 68 and 74-75.

[185] Petts, *Christianity in Roman Britain*, pp.118-120 and 124.

[186] J. Blair, *The church in Anglo-Saxon Society*, (OUP: Oxford, 2006) p.10.

[187] J. Morris (ed.) *Domesday Book: Huntingdonshire*, (Phillimore: Chichester, 1975) p.203c.

[188] S. Oosthuizen, 'Anglo-Saxon Monasteries and Minsters' in T. Kirby and S. Oosthuizen, (eds.) *An Atlas of Cambridgeshire and Huntingdonshire History*, (Anglia Polytechnic University: Cambridge, 2000) p.28.

[189] C. Platt, *The parish churches of medieval England*, (Chancellor Press: London, 1995) p.1.

[190] Cambridgeshire County Council Sites and Monuments Record, SM11550.

[191] The results of the excavation were published by the Museum of London in 2007. Merton Priory Trust (www.mertonpriory.org) was formed in 2003 and is seeking to establish a Heritage Centre to make the history of the Priory more widely available.

[192] N. Pevsner, *The Buildings of England: Bedfordshire, Huntingdon and Peterborough*, (Penguin: Harmondsworth, 1968) p.189.

[193] Lloyd argues that the letters WS on one of the misericords refers to William Stevens who was Vicar from 1470-1481. M. Wickes, *A History of Huntingdonshire*, (Phillimore: Chichester, 1985) p.49; D. Lloyd, *Historic Towns of East Anglia*, (Gollancz: London, 1989) p.184.

[194] J. F. D. Shrewsbury, *A history of bubonic plague in the British Isles*, (CUP: Cambridge, 2005) p.102.

[195] E. Duffy, *The stripping of the altars*, (Yale: New Haven, 1992) p. 355.

[196] Platt, *The parish churches of medieval England*, p.108.

[197] Rents received from obit lands 1548, Public Record Office MS DL38/5.

[198] R. Fox, *The history of Godmanchester*, (Baldwin and Cradock: London, 1831) p.254.

[199] Fox, *The history of Godmanchester*, p.268.

[200] C. Hicks, *Cambridgeshire Churches*, (Paul Watkins: Stamford, 1997) p.122.

[201] Huntingdonshire Archives, HP 34/4/1.

[202] Huntingdonshire Archives, HP 34/5.

[203] Huntingdonshire Archives, HP 34/5/2 and HP 34/5/9.

[204] Sir Edward Burne-Jones worked with William Morris on the designs.

[205] The prison building was demolished in 1928/9, and the site is now occupied by Shire Hall. Bricks from the prison were used in its walls.

[206] C. Gittings, 'Probate accounts: a neglected source', *The Local Historian*, 21 (1991), 51-59, p.53.

[207] C. Gittings, *Death, burial and the individual in early modern England*, (Croom Helm: London, 1984) p.97.

[208] D. Cressy, *Birth, marriage and death*, (OUP: Oxford, 1997) pp.444-7.

[209] M. Pitts, 'Compassion revealed in Quaker finds', *British Archaeology*, 95 (2007), p.6.

[210] Huntingdonshire Archives, Great Gransden Overseers of the Poor accounts HP 36/12/1.

[211] Huntingdonshire Archives, Godmanchester Overseers of the Poor accounts, HP 34/12/2/1; Kimbolton Overseers of the Poor accounts, HP 52/12/5.

[212] H. Mytum, *Mortuary monuments and burial grounds of the historic period*, (Springer: New York, 2007) p.14.

[213] R. Houlbrooke, 'The age of decency 1660-1760', in P. C. Jupp and C. Gittings, *Death in England: an illustrated history*, (Manchester University Press: Manchester, 1999) p.188.

[214] Cressy, *Birth, marriage and death*, p.428.

[215] C. Willett and P. Cunnington, *The history of underclothes*, (Dover: New York, 1992) p.55.

[216] G. Kitson Clark, *The making of Victorian England*, (Methuen: London, 1962) p.149.

[217] Huntingdonshire Archives, HO 129/176.

[218] Bird, *Memorials of Godmanchester*, III.

[219] Green, *Godmanchester*, p.46.

[220] Bird, *Memorials of Godmanchester*, III.

[221] Godmanchester Baptist Church Annual Report for year ended 31 December 2008.

[222] *Hunts Post* November 1916.

[223] Huntingdonshire Archives PH35/15

[224] Huntingdonshire Archives, D347/1/2: Church book *1819-1882*; D347/1/3: Church book *1882-1951*.

[225] Huntingdonshire Archives PH35/16

[226] *Hunts Post* 8 December 1916.

[227] *Hunts Post* 28 July 1916.

[228] P. Dandelion, *An introduction to Quakerism*, (CUP: Cambridge, 2007) pp.13-18.

[229] D. Shorney, *Protestant nonconformity and Roman Catholicism*, (Public Record Office Publications: London, 1996) p.14.

[230] Bird, *Memorials of Godmanchester*, III.

[231] Dandelion, *An introduction to Quakerism*, p.178.

[232] Wickes, *A history of Huntingdonshire*, p.97.

[233] Bird, *Memorials of Godmanchester*, III.

[234] Huntingdonshire Archives, Whitney Collection WH 1/153.

[235] *Hunts Post* 24 March 1895.

[236] C., Brown, *The Death of Christian Britain*, (Routledge: London, 2001).

[237] *The Times* 28 November 2009.

[238] C. Field, D. Voas and S. McAndrew, *British Religion in numbers project* http://www.brin.ac.uk/figures/documents/RelAttendance19832008_001.xls last accessed 20 April 2010.

[239] 43% claimed to have no religion and 7% were adherents of non-Christian religions. M. Beckford, *Daily Telegraph* 16 December 2009, p.1.

[240] Social Trends, 2007, p.219.

[241] G. Davie, *Religion in Britain since 1945*, (Blackwell: Oxford, 1994) p.107.

CHAPTER 8: EDUCATION

[242] Page, Proby and Inskip Ladds, 'Parishes: Godmanchester', p.111.

[243] Evans, *The forging of the modern state*, pp.331 and 336.

[244] Huntingdonshire Archives, Town Council Resolution and letters concerning the Education Department establishment of School Board for Godmanchester, HP34/25/2/5.

[245] S. Broadberry, 'Human capital and skills' in R Floud and P Johnson, (eds.) *The Cambridge Economic History of Modern Britain Vol. II* (CUP: Cambridge, 2004) p.57.

[246] Wickes, *A history of Huntingdonshire*, p.103.

[247] Page, Proby and Inskip Ladds 'Parishes: Godmanchester' 1974, pp.112-113 and Fox, *The history of Godmanchester*, p.337.

[248] Orders for the better Regulation and discipline of the Grammar School.

[249] M. Abbott, *Lifecycles in England 1560-1720*, (Routledge: London, 1996) p.80.

[250] Page, Proby and Inskip Ladds, 'Parishes: Godmanchester', p.113.

[251] Fox, *The history of Godmanchester*, p.343.

[252] Huntingdonshire Archives, Governors' Minute Book 1850-1968, 19 September 1870 and 18 June 1879.

[253] Huntingdonshire Archives, Queen Elizabeth School Log Book 1872 – 1875.

[254] Huntingdonshire Archives, PH 35/40

[255] Huntingdonshire Archives, Governors Minute Book Huntingdonshire Archives HRO 3915.

[256] Pevsner, Green and the inscription under the porch window all incorrectly give the date of the new classroom as 1851. The Ordinance Survey map of 1886 shows no sign of a classroom extension. The annual inspector's report of 1898 noted that there is 'an absence of classroom accommodation'. The architect's estimate of November 1898 clearly outlines some of the heating and lighting requirements for the proposed new classroom. In January 1899, Henry Chamberlain, vicar of Godmanchester and chairman of the governors, wrote to the Ecclesiastical Commissioners in response to the Education Department's requirements to provide scholars with a classroom, requesting financial aid. An estimate had already been obtained two months earlier 'for the cost of adding a classroom to schoolhouse for £300 approx'.

[257] K. Thomas, 'The meaning of literacy in early modern England' in G. Baumann, (ed.), *The written word: literacy in transition*, (Clarendon: Oxford, 1986) p.102.

[258] S. Mendelson and P. Crawford, *Women in early modern England 1550-1720*, (OUP: Oxford, 1999) p.90.

[259] D. Cressy, *Literacy and the social order*, (CUP: Cambridge, 2006) p.51.

[260] R. Allen, *The British Industrial Revolution in Global Perspective*, (CUP: Cambridge, 2009) p.53.

CHAPTER 9: THE BUILT ENVIRONMENT

[261] N. J. G. Pounds, *Hearth and home: a history of material culture*, (Indiana University Press: Indiana, 1989) p.208.

[262] T. Arkell, 'Identifying regional variations from the hearth tax' *Local Historian* Vol..33 (2003) 148-174, pp.166-7.

[263] E. M. Davis, 'The taxable chimneys of Huntingdonshire in Cambridgeshire' in P.S. Barnwell and M. Airs (eds.) *Houses and the hearth tax: the later Stuart house and society*, (Council for British Archaeology: York, 2006) p.102.

[264] Letter to Emily Baumgartner 15 October 1859.

[265] *Hunts Post* August 1906.

[266] Huntingdonshire Archives, Whitney Collection WH3/349.

[267] Kelly's Directory: Huntingdonshire (Kelly's Directories Ltd: London, 1910) p.7.

[268] A. Kramish, *The Griffin: The Greatest Untold Espionage Story of World War II*, (Houghton Mifflin: Boston, 1986) p.168.

[269] Dr M. Echenique report to Huntingdon and Godmanchester Civic Society 10 March 1999.

[270] *Hunts Post* August 1906.

[271] Kelly's Directory: 1910, p.28.

[272] E. Lord, *Brewers and brewing in Huntingdonshire*, (EAH Press: Girton, 2008) p.51.

[273] Lord, *Brewers and brewing in Huntingdonshire*, p.84.

[274] *Hunts Post* 11 February 1916.

[275] R. Honeybone, 'The Riverside Mill, Godmanchester' in *Records of Huntingdonshire* Vol.3 No.2, (1993), 6-13, p.7.

[276] Honeybone, 'The Riverside Mill, Godmanchester', p.10.

[277] Honeybone, 'The Riverside Mill, Godmanchester', pp.10-12.

[278] M. Eiloart, *Huntingdon County Gaol and House of Correction*, (Fern House: Haddenham, 2009) p.11.

[279] Huntingdonshire Archives, Whitney Collection WH1/15.

CHAPTER 10: POVERTY, CRIME AND HEALTH

[280] S., Oosthuizen, 'The parish poorhouse' *Records of Huntingdonshire* (1985) 9-13.

[281] Bird, *Memorials of Godmanchester*, XII.

[282] Huntingdonshire Archives, KHP34/15/1/11.

[283] J. Black, *Eighteenth-Century Britain 1688-1783*, (Palgrave: Basingstoke, 2001) p.186.

[284] R Porter, *The Penguin Social History of Britain: English Society in the Eighteenth Century*, (Penguin: London, 2001) p.114.

CHAPTER 11: WAR AND CONFLICT

[285] D. Jones, *Summer of Blood; the Peasants' Revolt of 1381*, (Harper: London, 2009) p.178.

[286] S. Sadler, *A royal entertainment?:Huntingdon, August 1645*, (Cromwell Museum: Huntingdon, 1995) pp.10-11.

[287] Sadler, *A royal entertainment?* pp.13-14.

[288] Details of those who died can be found at:
http://www.roll-of-honour.org/Huntingdonshire/Godmanchester.html last accessed 2 June 2010.

[289] J. Bell, *Huntingdonshire Heroes of the First World War*, (Melvyn King: St Ives, 1998) p.38.

[290] *Hunts Post* 24 November 1916.

[291] *Hunts Post* 11 August 1916.

[292] A. Akeroyd and C. Clifford, *Huntingdonshire in the Second World War*, (Tempus: Stroud, 2007) pp.18 and 78.

[293] Akeroyd and Clifford, *Huntingdonshire in the Second World War*, p.18.

[294] Akeroyd and Clifford, *Huntingdonshire in the Second World War*, p.42.

[295] M Faulkner, *A village childhood*, (Just Print It: Huntingdon, 2004) pp.42-5.

[296] *Hunts Post* 24 October 1940 and 12 December 1940.

[297] *Hunts Post* 22 August 1940.

[298] *Hunts Post* 3 October 1940.

[299] *Hunts Post* 5 December 1940 and 12 December 1940.

[300] *Hunts Post* 10 May 1945 and 17 May 1945.

CHAPTER 12: LEISURE

[301] J. De Vries, 'The industrial revolution and the industrious revolution', *Journal of Economic History*, 54 (1994), 249-270; J. De Vries, *The industrious revolution: consumer behaviour and the household economy, 1650 to the present*, (CUP: Cambridge, 2008) p.122.

[302] E. Lord, *Investigating the twentieth century*, (Tempus: Stroud, 1999) p.75.

[303] *Britain in 2010*. Economic and Social Research Council p.66.

[304] Lord, *Investigating the twentieth century*, p.91.

[305] J. Stevenson, *British Society 1914-45*, (Penguin: London, 1984) p.396.

[306] *Hunts Post* 15 December 1916 and 17 November 1916.

[307] A. Akeroyd and C. Clifford, *Huntingdon: eight centuries of History*, (Breedon Books: Derby, 2004) pp. 67, 118 and 148.

[308] K. Thomas, *The Ends of Life*, (OUP: Oxford, 2009) p.52.

[309] Dunn, *The Book of Huntingdon*, p.67.

[310] Evans, *The Forging of the Modern State*, p.323.

[311] S. Jones, *Workers at Play: A Social and Economic History of Leisure 1918-1939*, (Routledge: London: 1986) p.35.

[312] Huntingdonshire Archives, Whitney Collection WH3/2710

[313] Huntingdonshire Archives HP34/30/2/7

[314] *Hunts Post* 23 February 1895.

[315] *Hunts Post* 20 June 1940.

[316] R. Latham and W. Matthews, *The Diary of Samuel Pepys Volume III*, (Bell: London, 1970) p.221.

[317] D. Hufford, 'Portholme: Huntingdon's Aerodrome and its Flying Men' *Records of Huntingdonshire* (1985) 26-32, p.29.

CHAPTER 13: GODMANCHESTER PEOPLE

[318] J. Morrill, 'The making of Oliver Cromwell' in J. Morrill (ed.) *Oliver Cromwell and the English Revolution*, (Longman: London, 1990) pp.38ff.

[319] T. Webster, *Stephen Marshall and Finchingfield*, (Essex Record Office: Chelmsford, 1994) p.1.

[320] Webster, *Stephen Marshall and Finchingfield*, p.3.

[321] David said, 'I would not put forth my hand against the Lord's anointed' I Samuel chapter 26 verse 23.

[322] The background is the hostility between Israel and the Moabites. The prophet Jeremiah proclaimed that the Moabites were under God's judgement. Destruction will overtake them and her land will be depopulated. Those who fail to carry out the judgement of Moab are cursed by God.

[323] R. Burn-Murdoch, *What's so special about Huntingdonshire*, (Friends of the Norris Museum: St Ives, 1996) p.31.

[324] Based on the texts 2 Peter chapter 1 verses 10-11 and John chapter 11 verse 25.

[325] Page, Proby and Inskip Ladds, *A History of the County of Huntingdon: Volume 2*, pp.286-296.

[326] Chapter 7.

[327] Huntingdonshire Archives, Whitney Collection WH3/103

[328] Members of Huntingdon U3A Local History Group, *The Huntingdon Institution* (Huntingdon, 2008) p.9.

[329] J. L. Middlemiss, *Fairground Steam Engines 1864-1934*, (Middlemiss: Godmanchester, 1999) preface.

LIST OF SUBSCRIBERS

The authors wish to record their thanks to the following subscribers who helped to fund this publication.

Tina and Sam Badni

Kate Barkshire

Andrew Baron (St Anne's School)

Josephine and Martin Becker

Ursula Bissell

Bev Brace

Maureen and Byrom Bramwell

Barbara Brett

David Brown

Michael Brown

Ros and Richard Brown

Jessica Brudenell

Roger Brudenell

Pat and Richard Butcher

David Butterworth

Daniel Cade

Cathy Cannizzo

Victoria Cannon

Ralph Clark

Malcolm Cohen

Terry Collier

Mary and David Cozens

J. Crimmin

Patricia Davies

Eileen Dolan

Seonaid Dudley

Ian Dunbavin

Beryl and Derek Durant

Anne and Simon Eardley

Lyn and Keith Edmonds

Ros and Derek Fletcher

Teresa Fowler

Keith Gabb

Elspeth Gibbon

Brian Goddard

Prisca Greenhow

Steve Gresswell

Kate Hadley

Diana Hagues

Colin Hardy

Trish Harewood

Rita Harris

Peter Hartwell

Shelley and Jim Heeley

Lynda and Peter Heseltine

Jennifer Hirsh

Helen and Tony Hollington

Alan Hooker

Bonnie Hooker

David Hufford

Colin Hyams

Tim Ireson

Liz and Peter Irving

Lowri Ann Jacobsen

Trafford James

Pat Jones

Pat and Mervyn Jones

Russell Jones

Sue and Mike Jordan

Judith Kay

Caroline Kesseler

Carol and Mike King

John Leach

Lorraine and Gordon Leach

Philippa Leipa
Dr S Lewis
Madelaine Liddiard
John Little
Anne and Charles Looker
Joan Lumley
Lyn and Peter Martin
Jacqueline Mealing
Ian Meiklejohn
Sue Miller
Carol Monks
Sandra and Roy Norris
J. O'Callaghan
Pela Otman
Sarah and David Owen
Jayne Paynter
Tony Pepper
Nigel Pithey
Valerie and Dave Porter
Mary and Ian Radford
Gerald Reeve
Charles Remington
Susi and Graham Reynolds
Audrey Rudd
Sheila Salmon
Ken Savage
Laurie Sice
Bridget Smith
Naomi, Esther and Silas Sneath
Paula and Trevor Sparling
Stephen Spencer
Mary and David Stokes
Clare and Simon Summers
Mary and Sandy Telford
Tef Tewfik
Biz and John Thackray
Elizabeth Thompson
Maureen Thompson

Sandra and Peter Tremlett
Christopher Vane Percy
David Viles
Alan Welton
Lynda Wilkes
Anne Wilson
Sarah and Graham Wilson
Jan Wilson
Beth and Steve Wiseman
Alan Wolfenden
Angela and Andrew Wright
Sue and Jonathon Young

MAP OF GODMANCHESTER

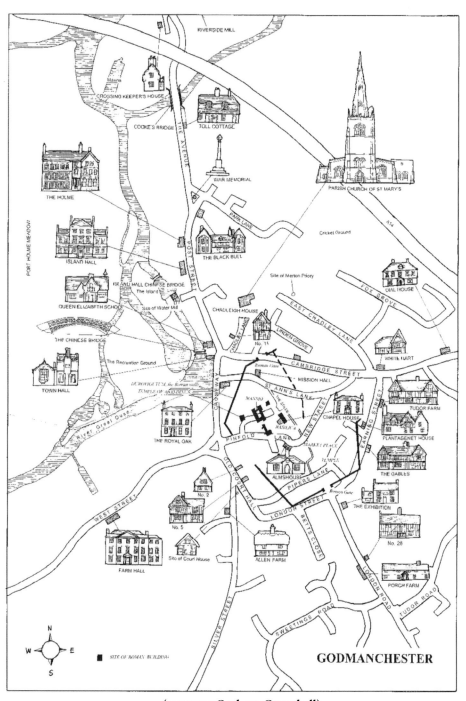

(courtesy Graham Campbell)

TIMELINE

Palaeo-lithic
- 950,000-500,000 Evidence of first pre *homo sapiens* hominids in Britain at Happisburgh, Pakefield and Boxgrove

Palaeo-lithic
- c.200,000 Evolution of modern humans in Africa
- 113,000 last interglacial period ended

Palaeo-lithic
- 100,000 Modern humans emerged from Africa
- 43,000 Modern humans arrived in Europe
- 18,000 last glacial maximum

Meso-lithic
- Ice retreats; The Ouse valley becomes an access route.
- 9600BC Hunter gatherers in Ouse Valley

Neolithic
- 4000BC development of farming. Wheat begins to be cultivated
- Temple of the sun built in Godmanchester

Bronze Age
- 2300BC first use of metal
- First field systems introduced
- Evidence of Bronze Age people in Roman Way

Iron Age
- Hill forts at Wandlebury and Arbury
- Godmanchester controlled by Catuvellauni
- 20BC Tasciovanus becomes King of Catuvellauni

Romans
- 43 Roman invasion; First fort built in Godmanchester
- 60-61 Revolt of Boudicca; second fort established
- 296 Major fire in Godmanchester

Anglo-Saxons
- Godmanchester a small hamlet
- Saxon domestic buildings outside town close to A1198
- Godmanchester controlled by Mercia

Danes
- 865 and 879 Danish raids and Godmanchester occupied by Guthrum
- 878 Guthrum defeated by Alfred at the Battle of Edington
- 917 Edward the Elder recaptured Godmanchester

Medieval
- 1066 Norman conquest
- 1086 Domesday Book
- Stephen (1135-1154) gave Godmanchester church to Merton Priory

Medieval
- 1190 Godmanchester granted to the Earl of Huntingdon
- **1212 King John's Charter**
- 1348-9 Black Death

Early Modern
- 1536-9 Dissolution of the Monasteries (including Merton Priory)
- 1561 Queen Elizabeth Grammar School established
- 1604 Charter of King James

Early Modern
- 1645 Charles I entered Huntingdon
- 1774 John Wesley preaches in Godmanchester
- Industrial and consumer revolutions

19th Century
- 1803 Godmanchester enclosed
- 1827 Town Chinese Bridge built
- 1828-30 Swing riots

19th Century
- 1847 Railways come to Godmanchester
- 1851 Religious census reveals strength of nonconformity
- 1870 Beginning of agricultural depression

20th Century
- 1903 Motor Car Act requires cars to be registered
- 1910 James Radley flies Bleriot monoplane on Portholme
- 1955 Godmanchester Junior School opens

20th Century
- 1977 Queen's Jubilee: Community Association established
- 1987 Wood Green Animal Shelter comes to Godmanchester
- 1994 Roman Gate surgery opens

GLOSSARY

Arminian A theological system named after Jacobus Arminius. It rejected the Calvinist doctrine of predestination.

Advowson The right to nominate a vicar or rector to a church.

Baptist Originating in the sixteenth century, Baptists believe that baptism should be restricted to adults and take the form of full immersion.

Basilica Town Hall and magistrate's court.

Borough English An inheritance system in which the youngest surviving male child inherits.

Calvinist Calvinists claim to follow the teachings of the Reformer John Calvin and emphasise the sovereignty of God. They believe in Predestination and reject the teachings of Arminianism.

Catuvellauni The most powerful Iron Age Tribe whose capital was at St Albans.

Enclosure The process of enclosing scattered strips of open fields into more manageable fields that were enclosed. This could be by agreement or by Act of Parliament.

Hearth Tax A tax based on the number of hearths in a property. Introduced in 1662 and abolished after William III became King in 1689.

Hide the area of land that a team of eight oxen could plough in a year, roughly 120 acres. A hide usually comprised four virgates (of 30 acres). A virgate (or yardland) was the size of a typical peasant farm.

Homo heidelbergensis *Homo heidelbergensis* lived from about 600,000 to 250,000 years ago and is probably the ancestor of modern man. The name derived from a heavy jawbone found near Heidelberg, Germany in 1908.

Homo sapiens Modern man.

Interglacial Period A warm period between two cold periods.

Lay subsidy A tax on moveable goods. In 1327 the rate was one shilling in the pound.

Magna Carta A charter of liberties conceded by King John in 1215 whilst under pressure from the barons.

Mansio Inn

Mesolithic The Middle stone age, beginning between 10,000BC and 8,000BC and ending around 4000BC.

Methodism Founded by John Wesley in the eighteenth century. Being Arminians, Methodists believe that salvation is possible for everyone and not just the elect.

Neanderthals *Homo Neanderthalensis,* a distinct human species from modern humans, lived in a large area of Europe and Asia from around 300,000 to 28,000 years ago.

Neolithic New Stone Age dating from about 4000BC to about 2300 BC.

Pigstel or pightle A small enclosure

Presbyterian A Calvinist Protestant church governed by presbyters or overseers. A moderating force during the Civil War when compared to other Protestant sects.

Puritan The 'hotter sort of Protestant' who wanted further reform of the Church of England. Strong supporters of Parliament in the Civil War but subsequently split into several sects.

Reredos A screen that stands behind the altar in a church, (also known as an altarpiece).

Secularisation The decline of religious values often associated with the rise of urban and industrial society.

Turnpike roads Toll roads administered by local trusts. Tolls were collected at turnpike gates.

Wics Trading ports or major centres of population in the Middle Saxon period.

DATING

The terms Mesolithic and Neolithic do not reflect an absolute dating system but relate to the period during which the relevant technology was practiced. Hence the Neolithic period in Huntingdonshire (3,500BC-2300BC) occurred much later than the Neolithic period in the Middle East.

FURTHER READING

Previously published works on Godmanchester in chronological order:

R. Fox, *The History of Godmanchester*, (Baldwin & Cradock: London, 1831)

F. W. Bird, *Memorials of Godmanchester*, (Peterborough Advertiser Company: Peterborough, 1911)

T. Pack, *A faithful standard bearer: exemplified in Thomas Stevens Freeman, who, amid unexampled persecution, formed the Particular Baptist Church at Godmanchester*, (Farncombe & Sons: London, 1931)

H. J. M. Green, *Godmanchester*, (Oleander Press: Cambridge, 1977)

J. A. Raftis, *Small Town in Late Mediaeval England, Godmanchester 1278-1400*, (Pontifical Institute of Medieval Studies: Toronto, 1982)

J. A. Raftis, *Early Tudor Godmanchester: Survivals and New Arrivals*, (Pontifical Institute of Medieval Studies: Toronto, 1990)

A. Jones, *Settlement, Burial and Industry in Roman Godmanchester: Excavations in the Extra-mural Area - The Parks 1998, London Road 1997-8 and Other Investigations*. Archaeological Reports British Series, (Archaeopress: Oxford, 2003)

Other important sources for Godmanchester include:

W. Page, G. Proby and S. Inskip Ladds, 'Parishes: Godmanchester', in *A History of the County of Huntingdon: Volume 2* Victoria County History (Institute of Historical Research: London, 1932)

M. Wickes, *A History of Huntingdonshire*, (Phillimore: Chichester, 1985)

F. Charles, *Operation Epsilon: The Farm Hall Transcripts*, (University of California Press: Berkeley, 1993)

T. Webster, *Stephen Marshall and Finchingfield* (Essex Record Office: Chelmsford, 1994)

T. Malim, *Stonea and the Roman Fens*, (Tempus: Stroud, 2005)

E. Lord, *Brewers and brewing in Huntingdonshire*, (EAH Press: Girton, 2008)

K. Sneath, *Consumption, wealth, indebtedness and social structure in early modern England*, University of Cambridge, 2009.

Various articles in *Huntingdonshire Records,* (Huntingdonshire Local History Society: Huntingdon, 1965-2011).

Godmanchester's web site (http://www.godmanchester.net) edited by Stuart Bond contains a wealth of historical information about the town.

INDEX